Welcome to *The Bourbon Table*
Bourbon-infused recipes from bite to bar
"Bourbon isn't just for sipping."

It started with a curiosity for whiskey — a neat pour here, a smoky dram there — but before long, I found myself down the rabbit hole of bourbon hunting. Suddenly, I wasn't just enjoying the occasional glass… I was tracking down rare bottles, learning mash bills by heart, and rearranging kitchen shelves to make room for a growing collection that might *technically* be encroaching on "obsession" territory. (My mother has since started gently asking if I'm "okay.")

But here's the truth: my love of bourbon was never just about the drink. I'm a cook at heart, and once I caught that first whiff of brown sugar and char coming off a bourbon reduction, I knew this spirit wasn't meant to stay in the glass. It belonged in the pan, the pastry, the glaze, the gravy — anywhere bold flavor was welcome. And so began my journey of folding bourbon into everything from comforting casseroles to decadent desserts, with a few happy hour nibbles along the way.

The Bourbon Table is where all that passion lives — the smoky, the saucy, the sweet, and the spirited. It's not about drinking more; it's about cooking with character. It's about capturing the depth of a well-aged pour and translating it into dishes that surprise, soothe, and satisfy.

So, grab a bottle (for cooking… or not), roll up your sleeves, and pour yourself into these pages. The bourbon's already waiting.

For my dad—

Mark Slocum 10/30/1960-06/25/2025

This book is his as much as it is mine. He was the one who first showed me that food is memory, that everything tastes better from scratch, and that cooking is love made tangible. Anyone who ever ate his famous nuggets knew how true that was. When he was sick, my care for him became the seed for this project, though I never imagined it would grow this far. He left us tasting every bourbon I could bring myself to share—and in the process, he gave me the confidence to believe my cooking was worth sharing with the world. None of this would exist without him, and I hope every page shows just how deeply he was loved.

People I'd Like to Thank

My bourbon fairy—for starting an addiction and feeding it generously when life was a little wild. Please also tell my mom (again) that bourbon hunting is a legitimate hobby in these parts.

My mom—who fell in love with my very first attempt at boozy baking: champagne cupcakes. That success gave me the courage to keep experimenting, and surprisingly, she's become the biggest champion of this book. I can't count how many times she's called to say she's pre-sold another copy. "Now when is it going to be published?!" Mostly, I just want to confirm that I'm not drinking all those bottles…

My husband—thank you for surviving the recipe testing, the flour explosions, the syrup-slick counters, and the bourbon runs. Thanks for not panicking when I get home from the liquor store and still helping me unload the car like a champ.

My stepfather—who likes to say he cooks with wine and sometimes even adds it in! Keep telling mom that for me! It may be why you're my favorite.

And to the rest of my family and friends—thank you for always encouraging me to do something with all that cooking, even if it was just making you a spare plate. I swear I'll drop off more cookies soon.

Distilleries I'd Like to Thank

(*But Who Haven't Noticed Me Yet*)

To the incredible bourbon makers behind the bottles that fueled these recipes (and, let's be honest, some of the decisions within them): I see you. I love you. Please respond to my emails.

Thank you for crafting spirits that taste like burnt sugar dreams and smell like campfire kisses. You've made my cooking better, my shelves fuller, and my mother *very* nervous.

This book would not exist without your delicious contributions to my kitchen — and my clutter.

Love,

    Your Unofficial, Unpaid, and Unrelentingly Loyal Hype Woman

P.S. Call me.

Barrel & Bite

Appetizers

These starters are where the cork pops and the party begins. With twenty bite-sized creations that swagger with bourbon in every crunch, drizzle, and dip, this chapter proves the bottle belongs on the prep counter as much as behind the bar. From sticky-sweet wings that demand napkins to veggie bites kissed with barrel smoke, each recipe invites you to pour a dram, pass the plate, and settle into that slow Kentucky glow.

Recipes in this chapter:

- Shrimp with Bourbon Garlic Butter
- Crab Cakes with Spicy Bourbon Remoulade
- Smoked Salmon Bourbon Spread
- Bourbon Tomato Bruschetta
- Bourbon Sausage Bites
- Bourbon-Glazed Meatballs
- Mini Bourbon BBQ Sliders
- Bacon-Wrapped Asparagus with Bourbon Glaze
- Whiskey Wings with Sticky Bourbon Sauce
- Mini Pulled Pork Sliders
- Deviled Eggs with Bourbon Mustard
- Stuffed Mushrooms with Bourbon Cream
- Bourbon Jalapeño Poppers
- Barrel-Battered Onion Rings
- Bourbon BBQ Flatbread Squares
- Boozy Bourbon Cheese Dip
- Bourbon Spinach & Artichoke Dip
- Bourbon Mac & Cheese Bites
- Bourbon Bacon Jam Crostini
- Candied Bourbon Bacon Strips

Shrimp with Bourbon Garlic Butter

Plump shrimp bathed in sizzling bourbon-garlic butter that begs for bread to mop it up.

Ingredients

1 lb (450 g) shrimp, peeled & deveined

3 cloves garlic, minced

Juice of ½ lemon

Salt & pepper, to taste

3 tbsp (45 g) unsalted butter

3 tbsp (45 ml) bourbon

2 tbsp (8 g) chopped parsley

Instructions

1. Pat shrimp dry, season lightly.
2. Melt butter in skillet, add garlic 1 min.
3. Add shrimp, cook 2 min per side.
4. Pour in bourbon, reduce slightly.
5. Finish with lemon juice & parsley.

Bourbon Pairings

Elijah Craig Small Batch warms with spice that echoes the butter, Maker's Mark keeps things caramel-smooth, and Four Roses Single Barrel brightens with fruit and vanilla.

Cocktail Pairing: Bourbon Lemon Smash

Bourbon, lemon, and mint shaken over ice — zesty enough to cut the butter's richness.

Warning: you'll want to drink the sauce — I won't judge if you do.

Crab Cakes with Spicy Bourbon Remoulade

Golden, crispy crab cakes topped with a creamy, boozy kick that says Maryland meets Kentucky.

Ingredients

1 lb (450 g) lump crab meat

½ cup (60 g) breadcrumbs

¼ cup (60 g) mayonnaise

1 egg, lightly beaten

1 tbsp Dijon mustard

1 tbsp Worcestershire sauce

1 tsp Old Bay seasoning

2 tbsp (30 ml) bourbon

Oil, for frying

Remoulade

½ cup (120 g) mayonnaise

2 tbsp (30 g) ketchup

1 tbsp bourbon

1 tsp hot sauce

1 tsp smoked paprika

Instructions

1. Mix crab meat, breadcrumbs, mayo, egg, mustard, Worcestershire, Old Bay, and bourbon. Form 8 patties.
2. Heat oil, fry crab cakes 3–4 min per side until golden.
3. Mix remoulade ingredients, chill.
4. Serve crab cakes hot with spoonfuls of remoulade.

Bourbon Pairings

Wild Turkey 101 is bold enough for spice, Bulleit Bourbon adds peppery edge that matches seasoning, and Woodford Reserve's nutty depth flatters the crust.

Cocktail Pairing: Spicy Bourbon Bloody Mary

Tomato, lemon, hot sauce, and bourbon over ice — the ultimate brunch rescue.

Proof that crab cakes don't have to stay sober.

Smoked Salmon Bourbon Spread

A creamy, smoky spread that doubles as a dip — bourbon ties it all together in silky luxury.

Ingredients

8 oz (225 g) cream cheese, softened

4 oz (115 g) smoked salmon, chopped

2 tbsp (30 ml) bourbon

2 tbsp (30 g) sour cream

1 tbsp lemon juice

1 tbsp fresh dill, chopped

Crackers or bread, to serve

Instructions

1. Mix cream cheese, sour cream, bourbon, and lemon juice until smooth.
2. Fold in salmon and dill.
3. Chill 30 minutes, serve with crackers or toasted bread.

Bourbon Pairings

Knob Creek's oak and vanilla complement the smoke, Basil Hayden's spice keeps things lively, and Angel's Envy adds a fruity port-kissed lift.

Cocktail Pairing: Bourbon Dill Martini

Bourbon, dry vermouth, orange bitters, and fresh dill — savory, herbal, elegant.

You'll never look at plain cream cheese the same way again.

Bourbon Tomato Bruschetta

Ripe tomatoes tossed in bourbon-balsamic glaze and piled high on toasted bread.

Ingredients

1 baguette, sliced & toasted

2 tbsp olive oil

2 tbsp bourbon

2 tbsp fresh basil, chopped

3 cups (450 g) cherry tomatoes, diced

2 tbsp balsamic vinegar

2 cloves garlic, minced

Salt & pepper, to taste

Instructions

1. Heat olive oil, sauté garlic 1 min.
2. Add tomatoes, balsamic, bourbon, salt, and pepper. Cook 5 min.
3. Spoon over toasted baguette slices, garnish with basil.

Bourbon Pairings

Buffalo Trace's bright fruit notes enhance tomatoes, 1792 Small Batch adds caramel richness, Old Forester 100 kicks up spice in the glaze.

Cocktail Pairing: Bourbon Spritz

Bourbon, Aperol, soda water, and orange — light, bubbly, and tangy.

Technically a salad if you eat enough of them.

Bourbon Sausage Bites

Savory sausage glazed in bourbon barbecue sauce — guaranteed to vanish first from the platter.

Ingredients

1 lb (450 g) smoked sausage, cut bite-size

2 tbsp (30 ml) bourbon

½ cup (120 ml) bourbon barbecue sauce

Toothpicks, for serving

Instructions

1. Brown sausage slices in a skillet.
2. Stir in barbecue sauce and bourbon, simmer 5 min until glossy.
3. Serve hot with toothpicks.

Bourbon Pairings

Jim Beam Black matches the smoky caramel notes, Evan Williams Bottled-in-Bond cuts richness with proofy backbone, Maker's 46 lingers with warm baking spice.

Cocktail Pairing: Bourbon Mule

Bourbon, lime, and ginger beer in a copper mug — crisp and spicy.

Warning: they disappear faster than you can say "where'd the sausage go?"

Bourbon-Glazed Meatballs

Juicy meatballs simmered in a sticky bourbon glaze that's equal parts sweet, savory, and addictive.

Ingredients

1 lb (450 g) ground beef	½ lb (225 g) ground pork
½ cup (60 g) breadcrumbs	¼ cup (60 g) milk
1 egg, lightly beaten	2 cloves garlic, minced
1 tbsp Worcestershire sauce	1 tsp salt, ½ tsp pepper
½ cup (120 ml) ketchup	¼ cup (60 ml) bourbon
¼ cup (50 g) brown sugar	1 tbsp soy sauce

Instructions

1. Mix beef, pork, breadcrumbs, milk, egg, garlic, Worcestershire, salt, and pepper. Form 20–24 meatballs.
2. Bake at 400°F (200°C) for 18–20 min until cooked.
3. In a saucepan, whisk ketchup, bourbon, brown sugar, and soy. Simmer 5–7 min until thick.
4. Toss meatballs in glaze, serve hot.

Bourbon Pairings

Old Forester 1920 layers caramel and oak that match the glaze, Wild Turkey 101 cuts through with bold spice, and Maker's 46 adds warm vanilla sweetness.

Cocktail Pairing: Boulevardier

Bourbon, Campari, and sweet vermouth — bitter-sweet balance against sticky glaze.

Warning: once you pop one, twenty may follow.

Mini Bourbon BBQ Sliders

Little burgers stacked with bourbon barbecue sauce — tiny buns, big personality.

Ingredients

1 lb (450 g) ground beef

8–10 slider buns

1 tbsp (15 ml) bourbon

Pickles, lettuce, toppings as desired

1 tsp salt, ½ tsp pepper

½ cup (120 ml) bourbon BBQ sauce

4 oz (115 g) cheddar cheese, sliced

Instructions

1. Form beef into 8–10 small patties, season with salt and pepper.
2. Grill or pan-sear 3–4 min per side.
3. Warm barbecue sauce with bourbon.
4. Assemble buns with patty, cheese, sauce, and toppings.

Bourbon Pairings

Buffalo Trace adds caramel that lifts the smoky sauce, Four Roses Small Batch brings spice and fruit, and Knob Creek stands up to bold flavors.

Cocktail Pairing: Kentucky Mule

Bourbon, lime juice, ginger beer — sharp and fizzy to cut through meaty richness.

Because regular burgers are just too sober.

Bacon-Wrapped Asparagus with Bourbon Glaze

Smoky bacon meets tender asparagus, brushed with a glossy bourbon glaze.

Ingredients

1 bunch (450 g) asparagus, trimmed

10–12 slices bacon

¼ cup (60 ml) bourbon

¼ cup (50 g) brown sugar

2 tbsp (30 ml) soy sauce

1 tbsp Dijon mustard

1 tbsp olive oil

Salt & pepper, to taste

Instructions

1. Preheat oven to 400°F (200°C).
2. Wrap 3–4 asparagus spears with a strip of bacon; place seam-side down on sheet pan.
3. Mix bourbon, brown sugar, soy, mustard, and olive oil. Brush bundles.
4. Roast 20–25 min, basting halfway, until bacon crisp.

Bourbon Pairings

Eagle Rare's caramel smoothness balances salty bacon, Elijah Craig adds spice that sharpens asparagus, and Woodford Reserve highlights glaze sweetness.

Cocktail Pairing: Old Fashioned

Bourbon, sugar, bitters, and orange peel — classic match for smoky-sweet flavors.

Proof that vegetables can absolutely be sinful.

Whiskey Wings with Sticky Bourbon Sauce

Messy, saucy, finger-licking wings that taste like bourbon took flight.

Ingredients

2 lbs (900 g) chicken wings	1 tsp salt, ½ tsp pepper
½ cup (120 ml) ketchup	¼ cup (60 ml) bourbon
¼ cup (50 g) brown sugar	2 tbsp soy sauce
1 tbsp apple cider vinegar	1 tsp smoked paprika

Instructions

1. Season wings with salt and pepper, bake at 425°F (220°C) for 35–40 min until crispy.
2. Simmer ketchup, bourbon, brown sugar, soy, vinegar, and paprika 10 min until thick.
3. Toss wings in sauce, serve sticky and hot.

Bourbon Pairings

Wild Turkey Rare Breed powers through spice and sauce, Bulleit Bourbon echoes smoky paprika, and Heaven Hill 7-Year layers in oak depth.

Cocktail Pairing: Bourbon Smash

Bourbon, mint, lemon, and sugar muddled — refreshing enough to reset between bites.

These wings demand napkins — lots of them.

Mini Pulled Pork Sliders

Slow-braised pork, shredded and piled high on slider buns with a bourbon kick.

Ingredients

2 lbs (900 g) pork shoulder

½ cup (120 ml) bourbon BBQ sauce

1 onion, chopped

1 tbsp apple cider vinegar

1 cup (240 ml) chicken stock

¼ cup (60 ml) bourbon

3 cloves garlic, minced

Slider buns, for serving

Instructions

1. Place pork in slow cooker with stock, onion, garlic, vinegar, and bourbon. Cook low 8 hrs until tender.
2. Shred pork, mix with BBQ sauce.
3. Pile onto slider buns, serve hot.

Bourbon Pairings

Maker's Mark soft caramel smooths the tangy sauce, Knob Creek stands bold against smoky pork, and Old Forester 100 adds a spicy backbone.

Cocktail Pairing: Bourbon Sweet Tea

Bourbon stirred into chilled sweet tea with lemon — Southern comfort in a glass.

Warning: impossible to eat just one.

Deviled Eggs with Bourbon Mustard

Classic deviled eggs, dressed up with a splash of bourbon and a mustardy kick.

Ingredients

12 hard-boiled eggs, peeled	¼ cup (60 g) mayonnaise
1 tbsp Dijon mustard	1 tbsp yellow mustard
1 tbsp bourbon	1 tsp hot sauce
Paprika, for garnish	Salt & pepper, to taste

Instructions

1. Slice eggs in half, scoop yolks into a bowl.
2. Mash yolks with mayo, mustard, bourbon, hot sauce, salt, and pepper.
3. Pipe or spoon filling into whites, sprinkle with paprika.

Bourbon Pairings

Larceny Bourbon's sweet wheat base smooths the mustard heat, Four Roses Small Batch adds floral spice, and Evan Williams Bottled-in-Bond keeps it bold.

Cocktail Pairing: Whiskey Sour

Bourbon, lemon, and simple syrup shaken to a froth — sharp enough to cut creamy yolks.

Hey Larceny: sponsor me, these eggs, and all our idle hands.

Stuffed Mushrooms with Bourbon Cream

Plump mushrooms filled with herby cheese, kissed with a bourbon cream finish.

Ingredients

16 large mushrooms, stems removed

¼ cup (25 g) Parmesan, grated

2 tbsp parsley, chopped

2 tbsp (30 ml) heavy cream

4 oz (115 g) cream cheese

2 cloves garlic, minced

2 tbsp (30 ml) bourbon

Salt & pepper, to taste

Instructions

1. Preheat oven to 375°F (190°C).
2. Mix cream cheese, Parmesan, garlic, parsley, salt, and pepper. Stuff mushrooms.
3. Place in baking dish, drizzle with bourbon and cream.
4. Bake 20 min until golden and bubbling.

Bourbon Pairings

Woodford Reserve's nutty oak fits mushrooms perfectly, Basil Hayden's spice keeps flavors lively, and Elijah Craig's caramel warmth makes it indulgent.

Cocktail Pairing: Manhattan

Bourbon, sweet vermouth, and bitters stirred smooth — dark, elegant, earthy to match the mushrooms.

Proof that fungi can be fancy.

Bourbon Jalapeño Poppers

Spicy jalapeños stuffed with creamy cheese, wrapped in bacon, and glazed with bourbon.

Ingredients

12 jalapeños, halved & seeded

1 cup (100 g) cheddar cheese, shredded

3 tbsp (45 ml) bourbon

8 oz (225 g) cream cheese

12 slices bacon

2 tbsp (30 g) brown sugar

Instructions

1. Preheat oven to 400°F (200°C).
2. Mix cream cheese and cheddar. Stuff jalapeños.
3. Wrap each with bacon, secure with toothpick.
4. Mix bourbon and sugar, brush over bacon.
5. Bake 20–25 min until bacon crisp.

Bourbon Pairings

Buffalo Trace balances sweet and spicy, Knob Creek doubles down with oak and heat, and Angel's Envy softens with a fruity finish.

Cocktail Pairing: Spicy Bourbon Margarita

Bourbon, lime, triple sec, jalapeño syrup — hot, tart, and boozy.

Warning: one bite and you're hooked.

Barrel-Battered Onion Rings

Golden onion rings fried crisp in a light, bourbon-spiked batter.

Ingredients

2 large onions, sliced into rings

1½ cups (180 g) flour

1 cup (240 ml) beer

¼ cup (60 ml) bourbon

1 tsp baking powder

1 tsp paprika

1 tsp salt

Oil, for frying

Instructions

1. Whisk flour, beer, bourbon, baking powder, paprika, and salt until smooth.
2. Dip onion rings in batter, fry in hot oil until golden.
3. Drain on paper towels, serve hot.

Bourbon Pairings

Jim Beam Black echoes caramelized onion sweetness, Old Forester 100 punches through with spice, and Maker's 46 lingers with warm vanilla.

Cocktail Pairing: Bourbon Shandy

Bourbon stirred into crisp lager with lemon — refreshing contrast to fried crunch.

If you're sharing, make a double batch.

Bourbon BBQ Flatbread Squares

Cheesy flatbread layered with tangy bourbon BBQ sauce and smoky toppings.

Ingredients

2 flatbreads (store-bought or homemade)

½ cup (120 ml) bourbon BBQ sauce

2 tbsp (30 ml) bourbon

1 cup (100 g) mozzarella cheese, shredded

½ cup (50 g) cheddar cheese, shredded

½ red onion, thinly sliced

½ cup cooked chicken or bacon bits

2 tbsp scallions, sliced

Instructions

1. Preheat oven to 425°F (220°C).
2. Spread flatbreads with BBQ sauce mixed with bourbon.
3. Top with cheeses, onion, chicken or bacon.
4. Bake 8–10 min until bubbly.
5. Sprinkle with scallions, cut into squares.

Bourbon Pairings

Wild Turkey 101 pops with bold spice, Elijah Craig ties smoke to sweetness, and Four Roses Small Batch adds fruit to balance tang.

Cocktail Pairing: Bourbon Smash

Bourbon muddled with lemon, sugar, and mint — crisp relief from cheesy richness.

Flatbread, but make it barrel-aged.

Boozy Bourbon Cheese Dip

Hot, melty, and dangerously easy to eat — bourbon takes classic cheese dip up a notch.

Ingredients

2 tbsp (30 g) butter	2 tbsp (15 g) flour
1 cup (240 ml) milk	½ cup (120 ml) beer
2 tbsp (30 ml) bourbon	2 cups (200 g) sharp cheddar, shredded
½ tsp smoked paprika	Salt & pepper, to taste

Instructions

1. Melt butter, whisk in flour 1–2 min.
2. Slowly whisk in milk, beer, and bourbon; cook until thickened.
3. Stir in cheddar, paprika, salt, and pepper until smooth.
4. Serve warm with pretzels or chips.

Bourbon Pairings

Maker's Mark soft wheat finish balances sharp cheddar, Bulleit Bourbon adds peppery backbone, and Woodford Reserve smooths the smoky paprika.

Cocktail Pairing: Bourbon Beer Back

Shot of bourbon chased with cold lager — simple, classic, perfect with cheese.

Warning: may cause sudden crowding near the snack table.

Bourbon Spinach & Artichoke Dip

Creamy, cheesy, and loaded with greens — a party dip with a bourbon backbone.

Ingredients

8 oz (225 g) cream cheese, softened

½ cup (60 g) Parmesan, grated

1 cup (240 g) cooked spinach, squeezed dry

2 tbsp (30 ml) bourbon

½ cup (120 g) sour cream

1 cup (100 g) mozzarella, shredded

1 cup (240 g) artichoke hearts, chopped

2 cloves garlic, minced

Instructions

1. Preheat oven to 375°F (190°C).
2. Mix cream cheese, sour cream, Parmesan, mozzarella, spinach, artichokes, bourbon, and garlic.
3. Spread in baking dish, bake 20–25 min until golden and bubbling.

Bourbon Pairings

Elijah Craig balances smoky oak with creamy richness, Buffalo Trace brightens the greens with caramel fruit notes, and Basil Hayden's keeps it light and peppery.

Cocktail Pairing: Mint Julep

Bourbon, mint, and sugar over crushed ice — cooling contrast to a hot dip.

Vegetables were never this indulgent.

Bourbon Mac & Cheese Bites

Creamy macaroni baked into bite-sized cups, with a bourbon-kissed crunch.

Ingredients

2 cups (200 g) elbow macaroni, cooked

2 tbsp (15 g) flour

½ cup (120 ml) cream

2 cups (200 g) cheddar, shredded

1 egg, beaten

2 tbsp (30 g) butter

1 cup (240 ml) milk

¼ cup (60 ml) bourbon

½ cup (50 g) Parmesan, shredded

½ cup (60 g) breadcrumbs

Instructions

1. Preheat oven to 375°F (190°C).
2. Make roux with butter and flour, whisk in milk, cream, and bourbon.
3. Stir in cheeses until melted, mix with pasta.
4. Fold in egg, spoon into greased muffin tin, sprinkle with breadcrumbs.
5. Bake 20–25 min until golden.

Bourbon Pairings

Knob Creek stands strong against cheesy richness, Angel's Envy's fruity finish brightens the bite, and Old Forester 100 adds spicy backbone.

Cocktail Pairing: Bourbon Cola Highball

Simple, fizzy, nostalgic — the fast-food sidekick mac & cheese never had.

Mac, cheese, and bourbon walked into a bar — and never left.

Bourbon Bacon Jam Crostini

Sweet, smoky bacon jam spread over crisp bread — the cocktail party MVP.

Ingredients

1 lb (450 g) bacon, diced

3 cloves garlic, minced

¼ cup (60 ml) apple cider vinegar

1 baguette, sliced & toasted

1 onion, finely chopped

½ cup (100 g) brown sugar

¼ cup (60 ml) bourbon

Instructions

1. Cook bacon until crisp, remove excess fat.
2. Add onion and garlic, cook until soft.
3. Stir in sugar, vinegar, and bourbon; simmer until thick and jammy.
4. Spread on toasted baguette slices.

Bourbon Pairings

Eagle Rare enhances smoky-sweet bacon, Bulleit Bourbon's spice complements onion tang, and Maker's 46 brings warm vanilla notes.

Cocktail Pairing: Manhattan

Bourbon, vermouth, and bitters — smooth, elegant balance to a rich bite.

Jam isn't just for breakfast anymore.

Candied Bourbon Bacon Strips

Salty-sweet bacon strips lacquered with bourbon caramelization.

Ingredients

1 lb (450 g) thick-cut bacon

3 tbsp (45 ml) bourbon

½ cup (100 g) brown sugar

1 tsp cayenne pepper (optional)

Instructions

1. Preheat oven to 375°F (190°C).
2. Mix brown sugar, bourbon, and cayenne.
3. Lay bacon on parchment, brush with glaze.
4. Bake 20–25 min until crisp and caramelized.

Bourbon Pairings

Elijah Craig caramel spice deepens the sweetness, Wild Turkey 101 cuts with bold punch, and Buffalo Trace highlights salty balance.

Cocktail Pairing: Bourbon Espresso Martini

Bourbon, coffee liqueur, espresso — smoky, sweet, and sharp enough to keep the party going.

The bacon that made dessert jealous.

Ladle & Libation

Soups

Every bowl tells a story — and in this chapter, the plot twist is always bourbon.

Pull up a chair, wrap your hands around a warm bowl, and inhale the alchemy of slow-simmered stock meeting oak-aged bourbon. From lightning-quick weeknight chilis to weekend-long roux rituals, these twenty recipes prove the best way to tame winter—or celebrate a summer storm—is with a ladle in one hand and a lowball in the other. Sip, stir, repeat.

Recipes in this chapter:

- Bourbon Bacon Corn Chowder
- French Onion Soup with Bourbon Crouton Melt
- Bourbon Tomato Basil Soup
- Smoked Brisket & Bourbon Chili
- Bourbon Gumbo with Andouille & Shrimp
- Bourbon Pumpkin Bisque
- Bourbon Clam Chowder
- Bourbon Ramen with Soft Egg & Pork Belly
- Bourbon Chicken Noodle Soup
- Classic Bourbon Beef Stew

Bourbon Bacon Corn Chowder

Creamy, smoky, and sweet — summer corn cozies up with bourbon and bacon for year-round comfort.

Ingredients

6 slices bacon, diced

2 cloves garlic, minced

2 cups (480 ml) chicken stock

1 cup (240 ml) heavy cream

2 medium potatoes, diced

Salt & pepper, to taste

1 onion, chopped

3 cups (450 g) corn kernels (fresh or frozen)

1 cup (240 ml) milk

¼ cup (60 ml) bourbon

1 tsp thyme

Scallions, for garnish

Instructions

1. Cook bacon in a pot until crisp, remove, leaving drippings.
2. Add onion and garlic, sauté 2–3 min.
3. Stir in corn and potatoes, season with thyme, salt, and pepper.
4. Pour in stock, simmer until potatoes are tender, 12–15 min.
5. Stir in milk, cream, and bourbon. Simmer gently 5 min, return bacon, garnish with scallions.

Bourbon Pairings

Buffalo Trace sweet caramel notes echo the corn, Knob Creek layers smoke over bacon, and Elijah Craig Small Batch brings spice that cuts the cream.

Cocktail Pairing: Bourbon Milk Punch

Bourbon, milk, sugar, and vanilla shaken with ice — a creamy nod to this chowder's richness.

This soup alone could start a bacon cult.

French Onion Soup with Bourbon Crouton Melt

Caramelized onions swimming in stock, crowned with bourbon-soaked bread and bubbling cheese.

Ingredients

4 large onions, thinly sliced

2 tbsp olive oil

½ cup (120 ml) bourbon

1 tsp thyme

Salt & pepper, to taste

2 cups (200 g) Gruyère cheese, shredded

3 tbsp (45 g) butter

2 cloves garlic, minced

8 cups (2 L) beef stock

1 bay leaf

1 baguette, sliced

Instructions

1. In a pot, melt butter with oil. Add onions, cook low and slow until caramelized, 25–30 min.
2. Stir in garlic, deglaze with bourbon.
3. Add beef stock, thyme, bay leaf. Simmer 20 min, season.
4. Top toasted baguette slices with Gruyère, float on soup bowls, broil until bubbly.

Bourbon Pairings

Maker's Mark caramel smoothness matches onion sweetness, Old Forester 100 cuts through with bold spice, and Woodford Reserve lingers nutty against the cheese.

Cocktail Pairing: Manhattan

Bourbon, vermouth, and bitters — smooth, rich, perfect alongside melted Gruyère.

Soup so good you'll forget it's basically just onions.

Bourbon Tomato Basil Soup

Bright, tangy, and silky with a splash of bourbon warmth — grilled cheese's soulmate.

Ingredients

2 tbsp olive oil

3 cloves garlic, minced

2 cups (480 ml) vegetable stock

1 cup (240 ml) heavy cream

½ cup (10 g) fresh basil, chopped

1 onion, chopped

2 cans (28 oz/800 g) crushed tomatoes

½ cup (120 ml) bourbon

1 tsp sugar

Salt & pepper, to taste

Instructions

1. Heat oil, sauté onion and garlic until soft.
2. Stir in tomatoes, stock, and bourbon; simmer 20 min.
3. Blend until smooth, return to pot.
4. Stir in cream, sugar, basil, salt, and pepper. Simmer gently.

Bourbon Pairings

Buffalo Trace caramel notes smooth acidity, Basil Hayden's spice keeps it lively, and 1792 Small Batch deepens the sweetness.

Cocktail Pairing: Bourbon Negroni

Bourbon, Campari, vermouth — bitter-sweet, cutting through the creamy tang.

Soup that turns a grilled cheese into a full-blown affair.

Smoked Brisket & Bourbon Chili

Deep, smoky chili with chunks of brisket, beans, and a bourbon-kissed sauce.

Ingredients

2 lbs (900 g) smoked brisket, cubed	2 tbsp oil
1 onion, chopped	3 cloves garlic, minced
2 bell peppers, diced	2 jalapeños, minced
2 cans (28 oz/800 g) crushed tomatoes	2 cups (480 ml) beef stock
½ cup (120 ml) bourbon	2 cans (30 oz/850 g) beans (kidney/black)
2 tbsp chili powder	1 tsp cumin
1 tsp smoked paprika	Salt & pepper, to taste

Instructions

1. Heat oil, sauté onion, garlic, and peppers.
2. Stir in brisket, cook until edges caramelize.
3. Add tomatoes, stock, bourbon, beans, and spices.
4. Simmer uncovered 45–60 min, stirring occasionally.

Bourbon Pairings

Wild Turkey Rare Breed matches chili heat with boldness, Elijah Craig adds caramel to tame spice, and Four Roses Single Barrel brings fruit that brightens smoke.

Cocktail Pairing: Bourbon Beer Boiler

Shot of bourbon dropped into a pint of dark beer — hearty enough for brisket.

This chili doesn't mess around — bring the big spoon.

Maple-Bourbon Butternut Squash Soup

Velvety squash soup layered with maple sweetness and bourbon warmth.

Ingredients

1 large butternut squash, peeled & cubed

2 tbsp olive oil

1 onion, chopped

3 cloves garlic, minced

4 cups (1 L) vegetable stock

½ cup (120 ml) bourbon

¼ cup (60 ml) maple syrup

1 cup (240 ml) heavy cream

½ tsp nutmeg

Salt & pepper, to taste

Instructions

1. Roast squash with olive oil at 400°F (200°C) for 25–30 min.
2. Sauté onion and garlic in pot, add roasted squash.
3. Stir in stock, bourbon, maple syrup; simmer 15 min.
4. Blend smooth, return to pot, stir in cream, nutmeg, salt, and pepper.

Bourbon Pairings

Woodford Reserve highlights maple richness, Angel's Envy adds fruity depth, and Maker's Mark keeps the finish buttery-smooth.

Cocktail Pairing: Maple Bourbon Old Fashioned

Bourbon, maple syrup, bitters, and orange peel — echoes the soup's sweet earthiness.

Basically, autumn in a bowl.

Bourbon Gumbo with Andouille & Shrimp

A Louisiana classic, slow-cooked with a bourbon-kissed roux.

Ingredients

½ cup (120 ml) oil

½ cup (60 g) flour

1 onion, chopped

1 bell pepper, chopped

2 celery stalks, chopped

3 cloves garlic, minced

1 lb (450 g) andouille sausage, sliced

1 lb (450 g) shrimp, peeled

6 cups (1.5 L) chicken stock

½ cup (120 ml) bourbon

2 tsp Cajun seasoning

2 bay leaves

Salt & pepper, to taste

Cooked rice, for serving

Instructions

1. Make roux: whisk oil and flour over medium heat until deep brown, 15–20 min.
2. Add onion, pepper, celery, garlic; cook until soft.
3. Stir in sausage, stock, bourbon, Cajun seasoning, bay leaves. Simmer 45 min.
4. Add shrimp last 5 min, cook until pink. Serve over rice.

Bourbon Pairings

Evan Williams Bottled-in-Bond cuts through richness, Four Roses Single Barrel adds fruity spice, and Knob Creek layers oak onto sausage smoke.

Cocktail Pairing: Sazerac (Bourbon Twist)

Bourbon, absinthe rinse, bitters, sugar cube — bold enough for gumbo's depth.

If bourbon met New Orleans, this would be the lovechild.

Bourbon Clam Chowder

A coastal classic with a bourbon splash that deepens every creamy bite.

Ingredients

4 slices bacon, diced

1 onion, chopped

2 stalks celery, diced

2 cloves garlic, minced

2 tbsp flour

3 cups (720 ml) clam juice

1 cup (240 ml) milk

1 cup (240 ml) heavy cream

½ cup (120 ml) bourbon

2 potatoes, diced

2 cups (300 g) chopped clams

Salt & pepper, to taste

Instructions

1. Cook bacon until crisp, remove. Sauté onion, celery, and garlic in drippings.
2. Stir in flour, cook 1 min. Add clam juice, milk, cream, bourbon, and potatoes.
3. Simmer until potatoes are tender, 15–20 min.
4. Stir in clams and bacon, cook 5 min more.

Bourbon Pairings

Buffalo Trace brightens briny clams, Elijah Craig's spice cuts the cream, and Basil Hayden's keeps things light and crisp.

Cocktail Pairing: Bourbon Bloody Caesar

Bourbon, clam-tomato juice, hot sauce, Worcestershire — briny, spicy, bold.

Proof that New England and Kentucky can share a bowl.

Bourbon Ramen with Soft Egg & Pork Belly

Rich broth laced with bourbon, noodles, smoky pork, and jammy eggs.

Ingredients

2 tbsp oil	1 onion, chopped
4 cloves garlic, minced	1 tbsp ginger, grated
6 cups (1.5 L) chicken stock	½ cup (120 ml) bourbon
3 tbsp soy sauce	2 tbsp miso paste
8 oz (225 g) ramen noodles	8 oz (225 g) pork belly, sliced
4 soft-boiled eggs, halved	Scallions & sesame seeds, for garnish

Instructions

1. Heat oil, sauté onion, garlic, and ginger.
2. Add stock, bourbon, soy, and miso. Simmer 20 min.
3. Cook noodles separately, divide among bowls.
4. Top with pork belly, soft egg, and broth. Garnish.

Bourbon Pairings

Evan Williams Bottled-in-Bond cuts through rich broth, Four Roses Small Batch adds floral spice, and Wild Turkey 101 carries the smoky pork.

Cocktail Pairing: Highball

Bourbon with soda water — crisp, bubbly, balances heavy broth.

If ramen grew up in Kentucky, this would be it.

Bourbon Chicken Noodle Soup

The ultimate comfort classic, reimagined with a bourbon backbone.

Ingredients

2 tbsp butter

1 onion, chopped

3 cloves garlic, minced

3 carrots, sliced

2 stalks celery, sliced

8 cups (2 L) chicken stock

½ cup (120 ml) bourbon

2 cups (300 g) cooked chicken, shredded

2 cups (150 g) egg noodles

1 bay leaf

1 tsp thyme

Salt & pepper, to taste

Instructions

1. Melt butter in pot, sauté onion, garlic, carrots, and celery 5 min.
2. Add stock, bourbon, bay leaf, and thyme; simmer 15 min.
3. Stir in chicken and noodles, cook until noodles tender, 10 min.
4. Remove bay leaf, season to taste.

Bourbon Pairings

Buffalo Trace's caramel smooths the stock, Knob Creek adds smoky backbone, and Maker's Mark ties it all together with sweetness.

Cocktail Pairing: Hot Toddy

Bourbon, honey, lemon, and hot water — the sip to cure whatever ails you.

Grandma's cure, with a Kentucky prescription.

Classic Bourbon Beef Stew

Hearty beef and root vegetables simmered low and slow with a bourbon twist.

Ingredients

2 lbs (900 g) beef chuck, cubed

2 tbsp oil

2 tbsp flour

1 onion, chopped

3 cloves garlic, minced

2 carrots, chopped

2 potatoes, cubed

2 cups (480 ml) beef stock

1 cup (240 ml) red wine

½ cup (120 ml) bourbon

2 tbsp tomato paste

2 sprigs thyme

2 sprigs rosemary

Salt & pepper, to taste

Instructions

1. Toss beef in flour, season. Brown in oil, remove.
2. Sauté onion and garlic, stir in tomato paste. Deglaze with wine and bourbon.
3. Add beef, stock, carrots, potatoes, thyme, and rosemary.
4. Simmer covered 2 hrs until beef tender.

Bourbon Pairings

Elijah Craig's spice deepens the broth, Wild Turkey 101 powers through richness, and Four Roses Small Batch brightens the finish.

Cocktail Pairing: Manhattan

Bourbon, vermouth, bitters — classic with a classic.

Cold night? This is your bowl.

Mash & Mains

Entrees

Welcome to *Mash & Mains*—the chapter where dinner classics get a double-barreled remix. Think sears that singe, braises that beg patience, and weeknight cheats that taste like Saturday night. From cast-iron crunch to slow-cooker swagger, every plate here gets seasoned twice—once with salt, and once with a splash of bourbon. Grab a fork (and a rocks glass) and dig in.

Recipes in This Chapter

- Bourbon Braised Short Ribs
- Bourbon Pot Roast
- Bourbon Chipotle Carne Asada Tacos
- Creamy Bourbon Chicken & Mushroom Tortellini
- Bourbon Beef Stroganoff
- Bourbon Shepherd's Pie
- Maple-Bourbon Glazed Salmon
- Soy-Bourbon Glazed Chicken Thighs
- Peppercorn Bourbon Steak
- Bourbon Fried Chicken
- Bourbon Jambalaya
- Bourbon Meatloaf
- Bourbon Chili Mac
- Bourbon Chicken Pot Pie
- Bourbon Carbonara
- Bourbon BBQ Ribs
- Duck à l'Orange with Bourbon Glaze
- Bourbon Honey Garlic Glazed Ham
- Bourbon Cajun Blackened Catfish
- Bourbon Stuffed Peppers

Bourbon Braised Short Ribs

Fall-off-the-bone short ribs simmered low and slow in a bourbon-kissed sauce until rich, velvety, and soul-hugging.

Ingredients

4 lbs (1.8 kg) bone-in short ribs

Salt & pepper

2 tbsp oil

1 onion, diced

2 celery stalks, chopped

2 tbsp tomato paste

2 cups (480 ml) beef stock

1 cup (240 ml) bourbon

2 carrots, chopped

3 sprigs fresh thyme

Instructions

1. Season ribs generously with salt and pepper.
2. Heat oil in Dutch oven; sear ribs on all sides until browned. Remove.
3. Add onion, carrots, celery; sauté until softened.
4. Stir in tomato paste, then deglaze with bourbon.
5. Return ribs, add stock, and tuck in thyme.
6. Cover and braise at 325°F (160°C) for 2½–3 hours until fork tender.

Barrel Picks

- **Woodford Reserve:** Its nutty vanilla backbone balances the richness of the ribs.
- **Elijah Craig Small Batch:** Toasty oak layers enhance the braise's depth.
- **Maker's Mark:** Soft wheat sweetness smooths out the bold beef flavors.

Cocktail Match — Smoked Old Fashioned

The smoky citrus twist mirrors the ribs' depth.

- 2 oz bourbon, ½ oz simple syrup, 2 dashes bitters.
- Stir over ice, strain into smoked glass, garnish with orange peel.

Proof patience—and bourbon—pays off.

Bourbon Pot Roast

Classic comfort with carrots, onions, and potatoes braised in a rich bourbon broth.

Ingredients

3–4 lb (1.5–1.8 kg) chuck roast

Salt & pepper

2 tbsp oil

1 onion, sliced

2 cloves garlic, minced

2 cups (480 ml) beef stock

1 cup (240 ml) bourbon

1 lb (450 g) potatoes, quartered

3 carrots, cut in chunks

2 sprigs rosemary

Instructions

1. Season roast, sear in hot oil until browned.
2. Remove meat; sauté onion, carrot, garlic.
3. Deglaze with bourbon, add stock and rosemary.
4. Return roast and potatoes to pot.
5. Cover and braise at 325°F (160°C) for 3–3½ hours.

Barrel Picks

- **Four Roses Small Batch:** Balanced spice weaves into the stew.
- **Bulleit Bourbon:** Bold rye edge brightens the hearty base.
- **Wild Turkey 101:** Its punchy proof cuts through the richness.

Cocktail Match — Boulevardier

A whiskey Negroni that sharpens the roast's deep flavors.

- 1 oz bourbon, 1 oz Campari, 1 oz sweet vermouth.
- Stir over ice, strain, garnish with orange twist.

Proof Sunday dinner is better with a splash of barrel.

Bourbon Chipotle Carne Asada Tacos

Smoky, spicy, and just boozy enough to deserve their own fiesta.

Ingredients

½ cup bourbon	Juice of 2 limes
2 cloves garlic, minced	1 tsp cumin
Salt & pepper	Tortillas & toppings

Instructions

1. Whisk bourbon, lime, garlic, chipotle, cumin, salt, pepper.
2. Marinate steak 2–4 hours.
3. Grill over high heat to desired doneness. Rest 5 minutes.
4. Slice thinly, serve in tortillas with toppings.

Barrel Picks

- **Four Roses Small Batch:** Its floral spice plays with chipotle heat.
- **Wild Turkey 101:** Stands tall against smoky beef.
- **Old Forester 100:** Bold caramel sweetens the spice.

Cocktail Match — Bourbon Margarita

The lime brightens the bourbon warmth while echoing taco zest.

- 2 oz bourbon, 1 oz lime juice, ½ oz triple sec, ½ oz agave.
- Shake with ice, serve in salted-rim glass.

These tacos bring the party—and the barrel.

Creamy Bourbon Chicken & Mushroom Tortellini

Plump pasta tossed in a luscious cream sauce, bourbon's oak sweetness elevating earthy mushrooms.

Ingredients

1 lb (450 g) cheese tortellini

2 tbsp butter

1 lb (450 g) chicken breast, cubed

8 oz (225 g) mushrooms, sliced

Salt & pepper, to taste

½ cup (120 ml) bourbon

1 cup (240 ml) cream

½ cup (50 g) parmesan

2 cloves garlic, minced

Parsley, for garnish

Instructions

1. Cook tortellini per package; set aside.
2. In skillet, sauté chicken in butter until browned; remove.
3. Add mushrooms, garlic; cook until tender.
4. Deglaze pan with bourbon, simmer 2 minutes.
5. Stir in cream, parmesan, and chicken; simmer until thick.
6. Toss with tortellini, garnish with parsley.

Barrel Picks

- **Buffalo Trace:** Subtle spice complements creamy richness.
- **Knob Creek 9 Year:** Bold oak matches the mushrooms' earthiness.
- **Angel's Envy:** Its port finish softens the savory bite.

Cocktail Match — Paper Plane

This modern bourbon sour brightens the dish with citrusy lift.

- ¾ oz bourbon, ¾ oz Aperol, ¾ oz Amaro Nonino, ¾ oz lemon juice.
- Shake with ice, strain into coupe.

Proof pasta deserves more than just wine.

Bourbon Beef Stroganoff

A classic comfort dish silked up with bourbon in the sauce.

Ingredients

1 lb egg noodles

1 lb beef sirloin, sliced

2 tbsp butter

1 onion, diced

1 cup mushrooms, sliced

½ cup bourbon

1 cup beef stock

1 cup sour cream

Salt & pepper

Parsley

Instructions

1. Cook noodles, set aside.
2. Sear beef in butter, remove.
3. Add onion, mushrooms; cook until soft.
4. Deglaze with bourbon, stir in stock.
5. Return beef, simmer 10 minutes.
6. Off heat, stir in sour cream. Serve over noodles with parsley.

Barrel Picks

- **Eagle Rare 10 Year:** Caramel layers deepen the sauce.
- **Wild Turkey Rare Breed:** Bold enough for creamy richness.
- **Larceny Small Batch:** Wheat sweetness softens mushroom bite.

Cocktail Match — Boulevardier

Bitter-sweet balance keeps the stroganoff rich but never heavy.

- 1 oz bourbon, 1 oz Campari, 1 oz sweet vermouth.
- Stir and serve over ice with orange peel.

Classic, creamy, and a little tipsy.

Bourbon Shepherd's Pie

Layers of savory beef, bourbon-rich gravy, and cheesy mashed potatoes baked golden.

Ingredients

2 lbs ground beef	2 tbsp butter
1 onion, diced	2 carrots, diced
1 cup peas	2 tbsp flour
½ cup bourbon	1 cup beef stock
2 lbs potatoes, boiled	½ cup milk
1 cup cheddar, shredded	Salt & pepper

Instructions

1. Sauté onion and carrots in butter until soft.
2. Add beef, season, cook through. Stir in flour.
3. Deglaze with bourbon, add stock, simmer 10 min. Stir in peas.
4. Mash potatoes with milk, cheddar, salt, pepper.
5. Spread beef mixture in casserole, top with potatoes.
6. Bake at 375°F (190°C) for 25 min until golden.

Barrel Picks

- **Jim Beam Black:** Smoky caramel enhances beefy depth.
- **Knob Creek 9 Year:** Oak warmth pairs with gravy richness.
- **Maker's 46:** Sweet spice lifts the creamy potato top.

Cocktail Match — Irish Mule (Bourbon Twist)

Bright ginger and lime keep this dish light on the palate.

- 2 oz bourbon, ½ oz lime, ginger beer.
- Build in copper mug with ice, garnish lime wedge.

Shepherd's pie, but make it barroom bold.

Maple-Bourbon Glazed Salmon

Sweet, sticky glaze meets buttery salmon for a weeknight showpiece.

Ingredients

4 salmon fillets

3 tbsp maple syrup

1 clove garlic, minced

Salt & pepper

¼ cup bourbon

2 tbsp soy sauce

1 tsp Dijon mustard

Lemon wedges

Instructions

1. Whisk bourbon, maple, soy, garlic, Dijon.
2. Marinate salmon 20–30 minutes.
3. Bake at 400°F (200°C) for 12–15 minutes, basting halfway.
4. Serve with lemon wedges.

Barrel Picks

- **Woodford Reserve Double Oaked:** Caramel-vanilla notes mirror maple.
- **Four Roses Single Barrel:** Spice offsets salmon's richness.
- **Angel's Envy:** Port finish pairs beautifully with glaze.

Cocktail Match — Maple Bourbon Smash

Herbal mint and maple make this salmon sing.

- 2 oz bourbon, ½ oz maple, ½ oz lemon, mint leaves.
- Shake, strain over ice, garnish mint sprig.

Weeknight ease, weekend flair.

Soy-Bourbon Glazed Chicken Thighs

Juicy chicken caramelized with sticky-sweet bourbon soy glaze.

Ingredients

6 bone-in chicken thighs

¼ cup soy sauce

2 cloves garlic, minced

1 tbsp oil

¼ cup bourbon

3 tbsp honey

1 tsp grated ginger

Sesame seeds, scallions

Instructions

1. Sear chicken in oil until golden. Remove.
2. Add garlic, ginger; sauté briefly.
3. Deglaze with bourbon, stir in soy, honey.
4. Return chicken, coat with glaze.
5. Bake at 375°F (190°C) for 25–30 minutes until done.
6. Garnish with sesame seeds and scallions.

Barrel Picks

- **Evan Williams Black Label:** Caramel backbone plays off soy and honey.
- **Elijah Craig Small Batch:** Toasted oak balances the glaze.
- **Bulleit Bourbon:** Bold spice highlights ginger.

Cocktail Match — Bourbon Highball

Bubbly and crisp to cut through sticky-sweet glaze.

- 2 oz bourbon, fill with club soda, lemon twist.

Sticky fingers, happy heart.

Peppercorn Bourbon Steak

A steakhouse classic with a fiery bourbon cream sauce.

Ingredients

2 ribeye steaks	Salt & pepper
2 tbsp butter	2 tbsp cracked peppercorns
½ cup bourbon	½ cup cream
½ cup beef stock	1 tbsp Dijon mustard

Instructions

1. Season steaks generously. Sear in butter to desired doneness. Remove, rest.
2. Add peppercorns to pan; toast 1 min.
3. Deglaze with bourbon, add stock, reduce by half.
4. Stir in cream and Dijon, simmer until thickened.
5. Spoon sauce over rested steaks.

Barrel Picks

- **Blanton's Single Barrel:** Vanilla-caramel smoothness tames pepper fire.
- **Wild Turkey 101:** Bold enough to match rich sauce.
- **Old Forester 1920:** High proof stands tall against ribeye.

Cocktail Match — Classic Sazerac

Strong, spicy, and herbal enough to rival peppercorn heat.

- 2 oz bourbon, ¼ oz absinthe rinse, 1 sugar cube, 2 dashes Peychaud's.
- Stir and serve in rocks glass with lemon twist.

This steak doesn't whisper—it roars.

Bourbon Fried Chicken

Crispy, juicy, and soaked in just enough bourbon buttermilk to make you blush.

Ingredients

1 whole chicken, cut pieces	2 cups buttermilk
½ cup bourbon	2 cups flour
1 tbsp paprika	1 tsp cayenne
2 tsp salt	Oil for frying

Instructions

1. Marinate chicken in buttermilk and bourbon overnight.
2. Mix flour, paprika, cayenne, salt.
3. Dredge chicken, shake off excess.
4. Fry in 350°F (175°C) oil until golden and cooked through (165°F internal).

Barrel Picks

- **Jim Beam White Label:** Classic, clean bourbon ties to buttermilk tang.
- **Knob Creek:** Bold spice pops against crispy coating.
- **Maker's Mark:** Wheat softness balances heat and crunch.

Cocktail Match — Sweet Tea Bourbon Punch

Southern comfort in a glass to match Southern comfort on a plate.

- 2 oz bourbon, 4 oz sweet tea, ½ oz lemon juice.
- Stir, serve over ice with lemon wheel.

If heaven had a crunch, it'd sound like this.

Bourbon Jambalaya

A New Orleans classic with a Kentucky kick.

Ingredients

1 lb andouille sausage, sliced

1 lb chicken thighs, diced

1 lb shrimp, peeled

2 tbsp oil

1 onion, diced

1 bell pepper, diced

2 celery stalks, diced

3 cloves garlic, minced

2 cups rice

1 can (14 oz) diced tomatoes

4 cups chicken stock

½ cup bourbon

2 tsp Cajun seasoning

Salt & pepper

Instructions

1. Brown sausage and chicken in oil; set aside.
2. Sauté onion, pepper, celery, and garlic until soft.
3. Stir in rice, tomatoes, stock, bourbon, and seasoning.
4. Add sausage and chicken back in; simmer 20 min.
5. Add shrimp; cook until pink. Adjust seasoning.

Barrel Picks

- **Wild Turkey 101:** Stands up to bold Cajun heat.
- **Buffalo Trace:** Caramel sweetness soothes spice.
- **Four Roses Small Batch:** Fruit and spice mingle with shrimp and sausage.

Cocktail Match — Bourbon Hurricane

A storm of fruit and spirit, perfect for Cajun feasts.

- 2 oz bourbon, 1 oz passionfruit juice, 1 oz orange juice, ½ oz lime, ½ oz grenadine.
- Shake, serve over ice with orange slice and cherry.

Bourbon meets the bayou.

Bourbon Meatloaf

Tender, glazed, and everything your mom made—only tipsier.

Ingredients

2 lbs ground beef	1 cup breadcrumbs
2 eggs	½ cup milk
1 onion, finely diced	2 cloves garlic, minced
½ cup ketchup	¼ cup bourbon
2 tbsp Worcestershire	1 tsp mustard
Salt & pepper	Parsley for garnish

Instructions

1. Mix beef, breadcrumbs, eggs, milk, onion, garlic, salt, pepper.
2. Shape into loaf, place in pan.
3. Stir ketchup, bourbon, Worcestershire, mustard for glaze.
4. Brush glaze over loaf.
5. Bake at 375°F (190°C) for 55–60 minutes.
6. Rest, slice, garnish parsley.

Barrel Picks

- **Old Forester 100:** Bold and classic to mirror comfort food roots.
- **Elijah Craig Small Batch:** Toasted oak and vanilla deepen glaze.
- **Maker's Mark:** Wheat sweetness echoes the ketchup-bourbon topping.

Cocktail Match — Boulevardier

Bourbon's richer cousin of the Negroni—bitters, sweet, and bold.

- 1 oz bourbon, 1 oz Campari, 1 oz sweet vermouth.
- Stir, strain over ice, garnish orange twist.

The loaf that learned how to party.

Bourbon Chili Mac

The comfort king: smoky chili meets cheesy mac, bound by bourbon warmth.

Ingredients

1 lb ground beef	1 onion, diced
2 cloves garlic	1 bell pepper, diced
1 can kidney beans	1 can diced tomatoes
2 cups beef stock	½ cup bourbon
2 tbsp chili powder	2 cups elbow macaroni
2 cups cheddar cheese	Salt & pepper

Instructions

1. Brown beef with onion, garlic, pepper. Drain fat.
2. Stir in beans, tomatoes, stock, bourbon, chili powder. Simmer 20 min.
3. Cook pasta separately until al dente.
4. Stir pasta into chili. Mix in cheese, season to taste.

Barrel Picks

- **Wild Turkey Rare Breed:** High proof cuts through chili heat.
- **Knob Creek:** Caramel richness ties meat, beans, and cheese.
- **Woodford Reserve:** Complex spice complements chili powder.

Cocktail Match — Bourbon Bloody Mary

Smoky-spicy sip to match hearty chili heat.

- 2 oz bourbon, 4 oz tomato juice, ½ oz lemon, hot sauce, Worcestershire.
- Shake, serve over ice, garnish celery + pickle spear.

Mac just found its swagger.

Bourbon Chicken Pot Pie

Flaky crust hides a creamy bourbon-kissed chicken filling.

Ingredients

2 cups cooked chicken, diced

2 carrots, diced

1 onion, diced

2 celery stalks, diced

2 tbsp butter

2 tbsp flour

½ cup bourbon

2 cups chicken stock

1 cup cream

1 cup peas

1 sheet puff pastry

Salt & pepper

Instructions

1. Sauté carrots, onion, celery in butter until soft.
2. Stir in flour; cook 1 min.
3. Deglaze with bourbon, whisk in stock, cream. Simmer to thicken.
4. Stir in chicken and peas. Season.
5. Pour filling into dish, cover with pastry.
6. Bake at 400°F (200°C) until golden, ~25 min.

Barrel Picks

- **Basil Hayden's:** Soft spice highlights creamy filling.
- **Eagle Rare:** Caramel-vanilla plays against buttery pastry.
- **1792 Small Batch:** Bold enough to keep balance with richness.

Cocktail Match — Hot Bourbon Cider

Sweet apple heat balances the savory pie.

- 2 oz bourbon, 6 oz hot apple cider, cinnamon stick.

The coziest blanket you'll ever eat.

Bourbon Carbonara

Pasta silked in egg, cheese, and just enough bourbon for a smoky wink.

Ingredients

12 oz spaghetti	4 oz pancetta
2 cloves garlic	3 eggs
1 cup	¼ cup
Parmesan	bourbon
2 tbsp butter	Salt & pepper

Instructions

1. Cook spaghetti until al dente; reserve ½ cup pasta water.
2. Cook pancetta with garlic until crisp. Remove garlic.
3. Whisk eggs, Parmesan, bourbon, pepper.
4. Toss pasta with pancetta, butter, egg mixture.
5. Add pasta water as needed to make creamy sauce.

Barrel Picks

- **Jefferson's Ocean:** Briny notes pair with pancetta and Parmesan.
- **Four Roses Small Batch Select:** Spice dances with garlic and cheese.
- **Maker's 46:** Sweetness balances bourbon's smoky depth.

Cocktail Match — Gold Rush

Bright honey-lemon lift to match rich pasta.

- 2 oz bourbon, ¾ oz lemon, ¾ oz honey syrup.
- Shake, serve over ice.

Italy called. Kentucky answered.

Bourbon BBQ Ribs

Sticky, smoky, and finger-licking proof bourbon belongs at the grill.

Ingredients

2 racks baby back ribs	1 cup bourbon BBQ sauce
½ cup bourbon	2 tbsp brown sugar
1 tbsp paprika	1 tbsp garlic powder
1 tbsp onion powder	Salt & pepper

Instructions

1. Mix spices; rub over ribs. Wrap in foil, refrigerate 1 hr.
2. Bake at 300°F (150°C) for 2½–3 hrs until tender.
3. Mix BBQ sauce with bourbon. Brush ribs generously.
4. Broil or grill briefly to caramelize glaze.

Barrel Picks

- **Knob Creek Single Barrel:** High proof stands up to rich glaze.
- **Elijah Craig Barrel Proof:** Bold caramel + oak play against smoke.
- **Maker's Mark 46:** Sweet-spicy balance enhances sticky sauce.

Cocktail Match — Smoked Old Fashioned

The classic cocktail with a BBQ twist.

- 2 oz bourbon, ¼ oz simple syrup, 2 dashes bitters. Stir.
- Strain over ice, garnish with orange peel + cherry. Smoke glass before serving.

Ribs you'll need a stack of napkins for—and a second pour.

Duck à l'Orange with Bourbon Glaze

A French classic in a bourbon tuxedo.

Ingredients

2 duck breasts

1 cup orange juice

2 tbsp honey

2 cloves garlic, minced

Salt & pepper

½ cup bourbon

Zest of 1 orange

1 tbsp soy sauce

1 tbsp butter

Fresh thyme

Instructions

1. Score duck skin, season. Sear skin-side down until crisp, ~6 min. Flip and cook 3–4 min.
2. Remove, rest. In pan, add garlic, bourbon, juice, zest, honey, soy. Reduce.
3. Whisk in butter. Slice duck, drizzle glaze, garnish thyme.

Barrel Picks

- **Woodford Reserve Double Oaked:** Caramel depth pairs with citrus glaze.
- **Angel's Envy:** Port finish complements duck's richness.
- **Baker's 7 Year:** Bold spice balances sweet orange-honey glaze.

Cocktail Match — Bourbon Sidecar

Elegant citrus echo.

- 2 oz bourbon, 1 oz orange liqueur, ¾ oz lemon juice.
- Shake, serve in coupe with sugared rim.

Duck never had it this smooth.

Bourbon Honey Garlic Glazed Ham

Holiday centerpiece meets everyday crave.

Ingredients

1 spiral-cut ham (8–10 lbs)

½ cup bourbon

1 cup honey

½ cup brown sugar

2 tbsp Dijon mustard

4 cloves garlic, minced

Instructions

1. Mix honey, bourbon, sugar, mustard, garlic.
2. Score ham, place in roasting pan. Brush with glaze.
3. Cover with foil; bake at 325°F (165°C) for 1½ hrs.
4. Remove foil, baste with glaze. Bake 30 more min.

Barrel Picks

- **Buffalo Trace:** Gentle caramel and spice complement honey sweetness.
- **Russell's Reserve 10 Year:** Oaky depth pairs with roasted ham.
- **Eagle Rare:** Smooth vanilla notes lift garlic-honey glaze.

Cocktail Match — Kentucky Mule

Crisp ginger sparkle keeps ham from getting too sweet.

- 2 oz bourbon, ½ oz lime, ginger beer to top.
- Serve in copper mug, garnish lime wedge.

Ham that steals the holiday spotlight—and Monday leftovers.

Bourbon Cajun Blackened Catfish

Smoky, spicy, and straight from the skillet.

Ingredients

4 catfish fillets	2 tbsp Cajun seasoning
2 tbsp oil	½ cup bourbon
1 lemon, juiced	2 tbsp butter
Fresh parsley	Salt & pepper

Instructions

1. Pat fillets dry. Rub with Cajun seasoning.
2. Heat oil in cast iron. Cook fish 2–3 min per side until blackened.
3. Deglaze with bourbon + lemon, add butter. Simmer briefly.
4. Spoon sauce over fillets, garnish parsley.

Barrel Picks

- **Wild Turkey 101:** Proof and spice punch through Cajun heat.
- **Four Roses Small Batch:** Fruity spice highlights blackened crust.
- **Old Forester 1920:** Dark, smoky depth matches skillet char.

Cocktail Match — Bourbon Lemonade

Refreshing counterpunch to spice.

- 2 oz bourbon, 4 oz lemonade, splash of soda.
- Serve tall with lemon wheel + mint sprig.

Spice, sear, and sizzle in every bite.

Bourbon Stuffed Peppers

A family favorite with bourbon warmth baked inside.

Ingredients

6 bell peppers, tops cut	1 lb ground beef
1 cup rice, cooked	1 onion, diced
2 cloves garlic, minced	1 can diced tomatoes
1 cup cheese	½ cup bourbon
1 tsp Italian seasoning	Salt & pepper

Instructions

1. Brown beef with onion, garlic. Stir in rice, tomatoes, bourbon, seasoning.
2. Stuff peppers with filling. Top with cheese.
3. Bake at 375°F (190°C) for 30–35 min.

Barrel Picks

- **Elijah Craig Small Batch:** Toasted caramel flavors echo roasted peppers.
- **Maker's Mark:** Wheat sweetness ties in tomato filling.
- **Bulleit Bourbon:** Bold spice balances hearty stuffing.

Cocktail Match — Bourbon Sangria

Light, fruity, and pepper-bright.

- 2 oz bourbon, 3 oz red wine, ½ oz orange liqueur, splash soda, fruit slices.

Comfort food, elevated with a pour.

Sauced & Spirited

Sauces

Sauce is the secret handshake of cooking—what turns "just food" into an experience. In these pages you'll find everything from silky dessert drizzles to hearty pan gravies, each one kissed by bourbon's rich warmth. Whether you're spooning a ripple of caramel over ice cream or deglazing a skillet for the juiciest steak, you're about to upgrade every bite with spirit and swagger.

Grab your whisk, heat your skillet, and let's get sauced.

Sweet Sauces & Dips

- Bourbon-Caramel Sauce

- Dark Chocolate Ganache

- Raspberry Bourbon Coulis

- Apple-Bourbon Compote

- Butterscotch Bourbon Sauce

Savory Sauces & Glazes

- Bourbon Onion Gravy

- Mushroom Bourbon Pan Sauce

- Bourbon BBQ Glaze

- Bourbon Bacon Jam

- Soy-Bourbon Glaze

Bourbon Caramel Sauce

Golden, glossy, and spiked with bourbon — the kind of sauce that makes plain ice cream taste like it belongs on a dessert menu.

Ingredients

1 cup (200 g) sugar

½ cup (120 ml) heavy cream

Pinch of sea salt

6 tbsp (85 g) unsalted butter, cubed

2 tbsp bourbon

Instructions

1. In a heavy saucepan, melt sugar over medium heat until amber and liquid, swirling gently.
2. Add butter carefully and whisk until melted.
3. Slowly pour in cream, whisking (mixture will bubble).
4. Stir in bourbon and salt.
5. Cool slightly before serving.

Pair it with bourbon:

- **Eagle Rare 10** — caramel notes high-five the sauce's buttery sweetness.
- **Buffalo Trace** — approachable, smooth, and vanilla-rich, perfect for desserts.
- **Elijah Craig Small Batch** — a warm oak finish that balances the sweetness.

Cocktail Match: Bourbon Milk Punch

Bourbon, milk, vanilla, and nutmeg shaken until frothy. Like caramel sauce in a glass.

A drizzle this good deserves a double pour.

Dark Chocolate Ganache

Smooth, shiny, and sinfully rich, this ganache turns any cake into a showstopper with just one swoop of the spoon.

Ingredients

8 oz (225 g) dark chocolate, chopped

2 tbsp bourbon

1 cup (240 ml) heavy cream

Pinch of salt

Instructions

1. Heat cream until just simmering, then pour over chocolate in a bowl.
2. Let sit 1–2 minutes, then whisk until smooth.
3. Stir in bourbon and salt.
4. Use warm for drizzling or chill for frosting/truffles.

Pair it with bourbon:

- **Booker's** — bold barrel proof that can stand toe-to-toe with dark chocolate.
- **Four Roses Small Batch Select** — layered spice complements the richness.
- **Maker's 46** — vanilla and caramel smooth out the bittersweet edge.

Cocktail Match: Manhattan

Bourbon, sweet vermouth, bitters, cherry garnish. A silky echo to the ganache's elegance.

Proof that chocolate has a drinking problem, and bourbon is the enabler.

Raspberry Bourbon Coulis

Bright and tangy with just enough barrel heat to keep things interesting, this coulis is a fruity counterpoint to all that sweetness.

Ingredients

2 cups (250 g) raspberries

½ cup (100 g) sugar

2 tbsp lemon juice

2 tbsp bourbon

Instructions

1. Simmer raspberries, sugar, and lemon juice over medium heat until soft.
2. Puree and strain through a fine sieve.
3. Stir in bourbon.
4. Chill before serving over cakes, cheesecakes, or ice cream.

Pair it with bourbon:

- **Bulleit** — spice meets tart berry zing.
- **Woodford Reserve** — balanced fruit and oak, a natural bridge.
- **Wild Turkey 101** — bold enough to cut through raspberry's brightness.

Cocktail Match: Bourbon Bramble

Bourbon, lemon juice, simple syrup, drizzle of blackberry liqueur. Fruity, tart, and fresh.

Coulis: the French word for "sauce that makes everything fancy."

Apple-Bourbon Compote

Tender apples simmered down with sugar, spice, and a splash of bourbon — a chunky, spoonable topping that's just as happy over pork chops as it is on pancakes.

Ingredients

4 apples, peeled & diced	¼ cup (50 g) brown sugar
1 tsp cinnamon	¼ tsp nutmeg
2 tbsp bourbon	1 tbsp butter

Instructions

1. Melt butter in skillet. Add apples, sugar, and spices.
2. Cook until tender and caramelized, about 10 minutes.
3. Stir in bourbon and cook 1–2 minutes.
4. Serve warm over pork chops, pancakes, or ice cream.

Pair it with bourbon:

- **Woodford Reserve Double Oaked** — apple pie in liquid form.
- **Buffalo Trace** — vanilla warmth that complements fruit.
- **Larceny** — wheated softness lets the apples shine.

Cocktail Match: Bourbon Apple Smash

Bourbon, muddled apple, lemon, and mint, topped with club soda. Crisp and orchard-fresh.

Proof that apple pie filling was always meant to be tipsy.

Butterscotch Bourbon Sauce

Buttery, brown sugar sweetness laced with bourbon's oak — a warm, nostalgic drizzle that tastes like comfort with a kick.

Ingredients

½ cup (115 g) butter

1 cup (200 g) brown sugar

1 cup (240 ml) heavy cream

2 tbsp bourbon

1 tsp vanilla extract

Pinch of salt

Instructions

1. Melt butter and sugar in saucepan, stirring until bubbly.
2. Slowly whisk in cream, cooking until smooth.
3. Stir in bourbon, vanilla, and salt.
4. Serve warm over bread pudding or ice cream.

Pair it with bourbon:

- **Old Forester 1920** — deep caramel echoes the butterscotch.
- **Elijah Craig Small Batch** — vanilla and spice, a classic match.
- **Four Roses Single Barrel** — floral sweetness to brighten the richness.

Cocktail Match: Brown Butter Old Fashioned

Bourbon infused with browned butter, stirred with sugar and bitters. Dessert in a rocks glass.

Butterscotch and bourbon: the duo your dentist dreads.

Bourbon Onion Gravy

Caramelized onions and bourbon team up for a rich, savory gravy that begs to be poured over everything in sight.

Ingredients

2 tbsp butter	2 large onions, thinly sliced
1 tbsp flour	1 cup (240 ml) beef stock
½ cup (120 ml) bourbon	1 tsp Worcestershire sauce
Salt & pepper, to taste	

Instructions

1. Melt butter, sauté onions until golden brown.
2. Stir in flour, cooking 1–2 minutes.
3. Slowly whisk in bourbon and stock.
4. Simmer until thickened, finish with Worcestershire.

Pair it with bourbon:

- **Jim Beam Black** — approachable oak flavor that echoes caramelized onions.
- **Wild Turkey 101** — bold spice to cut through savory richness.
- **Knob Creek 9** — high proof brings backbone to the gravy.

Cocktail Match: Manhattan

Bourbon, sweet vermouth, bitters, garnished with a cherry. A classic that loves onions on the side.

Gravy: the only acceptable excuse to drown your dinner.

Mushroom Bourbon Pan Sauce

Deep, earthy mushrooms lifted with a splash of bourbon — the skillet sauce that makes weeknight steakhouse-worthy.

Ingredients

2 tbsp butter	1 cup (150 g) mushrooms, sliced
1 shallot, minced	1 tbsp flour
½ cup (120 ml) bourbon	1 cup (240 ml) beef or chicken stock
1 tsp Dijon mustard	Salt & pepper to taste

Instructions

1. Cook mushrooms and shallots in butter until browned.
2. Stir in flour, cooking briefly.
3. Deglaze pan with bourbon.
4. Add stock and mustard; simmer until thickened.

Pair it with bourbon:

- **Woodford Reserve** — mushroom earthiness meets its oak vanilla.
- **Old Forester 1910** — double-barrel depth mirrors savory layers.
- **Maker's 46** — spice from seared oak complements umami.

Cocktail Match: Bourbon Sour

Bourbon, lemon juice, simple syrup. Tart enough to brighten earthy sauce.

Mushrooms and bourbon: earth meets fire in the skillet.

Bourbon BBQ Glaze

Smoky, sweet, sticky, and spiked — this is barbecue sauce with a barrel-aged soul.⸮

Ingredients

1 cup (240 ml) ketchup

¼ cup (60 ml) bourbon

1 tbsp Worcestershire sauce

1 tsp chili powder

Salt & pepper, to taste

¼ cup (50 g) brown sugar

2 tbsp apple cider vinegar

1 tsp smoked paprika

½ tsp garlic powder

Instructions

1. Combine all ingredients in saucepan.
2. Simmer 15–20 minutes until thickened.
3. Brush over ribs, chicken, or burgers while grilling.

Pair it with bourbon:

- **Wild Turkey Rare Breed** — bold spice keeps up with smoky BBQ.
- **Jack Daniel's Single Barrel (yes, the Tennessee cousin)** — caramel sweetness loves char.
- **Knob Creek Smoked Maple** — dessert-like smoke mirrors BBQ depth.

Cocktail Match: Kentucky Mule

Bourbon, ginger beer, lime. Refreshing fire extinguisher for smoky-spicy bites.

Warning: this glaze will cause spontaneous rib licking.

Bourbon Bacon Jam

Thick, spreadable magic made of smoky bacon, sweet onions, and a bourbon backbone — as good on toast as it is on burgers.

Ingredients

- 1 lb (450 g) bacon, chopped
- 2 large onions, diced
- ½ cup (100 g) brown sugar
- ½ cup (120 ml) bourbon
- ¼ cup (60 ml) apple cider vinegar
- 2 tbsp maple syrup
- 1 tsp smoked paprika
- ½ tsp chili flakes

Instructions

1. Cook bacon until crisp, remove and drain.
2. In rendered fat, sauté onions until soft.
3. Stir in sugar, vinegar, bourbon, maple, paprika, and chili flakes.
4. Simmer until thick and jammy; stir bacon back in.

Pair it with bourbon:

- **Booker's** — high proof stands tall against smoky-sweet jam.
- **Maker's Mark Cask Strength** — caramel richness makes the bacon sing.
- **Wild Turkey 101** — sturdy spice keeps jam from leaning too sweet.

Cocktail Match: Old Fashioned

Bourbon, sugar, bitters, orange peel. Classic, simple, bacon-approved.

Proof that bacon belongs in your fridge and your bar cart.

Soy-Bourbon Glaze

Salty-sweet with a flash of ginger heat, this glaze fuses Southern bourbon comfort with Asian-inspired flair.

Ingredients

½ cup (120 ml) soy sauce	¼ cup (60 ml) bourbon
¼ cup (50 g) brown sugar	2 tbsp honey
2 cloves garlic, minced	1 tsp fresh ginger, grated
1 tsp sesame oil	½ tsp red pepper flakes

Instructions

1. Whisk all ingredients in saucepan.
2. Simmer 10 minutes until glossy and thickened.
3. Brush over grilled chicken, salmon, or veggies.

Pair it with bourbon:

- **Four Roses Small Batch** — floral spice balances salty soy.
- **Elijah Craig Toasted Barrel** — smoky caramel depth fits Asian glaze.
- **Basil Hayden** — lighter body won't overpower delicate dishes.

Cocktail Match: Whiskey Ginger

Bourbon + ginger ale. Simple sparkle to mirror the glaze's sweet heat.

East meets South, and the handshake is delicious.

Smoke & Sugar

Desserts

Desserts are where bourbon really struts—sweet, sultry, and just a little unruly. From beginner-friendly cookies to flambéed finales, this chapter proves you don't need an excuse to end the night with spirit. Whether you're licking batter, torching meringue, or sipping something neat while the oven preheats, *Smoke & Sugar* is your decadent guide to unforgettable sweets.

- Citrus & Sin (Orange Curd Tart)
- Midnight Barrel (Dark Chocolate Torte)
- Cotta in the Act (Blood Orange Panna Cotta)
- Raspberry Flame (Baked Alaska)
- The Banana Stand (Banana Upside-Down Cake)
- Hole Lotta Bourbon (Glazed Donuts)
- Bourbon Snickerdoodles
- Cast Iron Kiss (Skillet Cookie)
- Easy Does It (No-Bake Mousse Cups)
- Bourbon-Pecan Shortbread Bars
- Whiskey Brownies
- Bourbon Bread Pudding
- Pumpkin Crème Brûlée
- Peach Raspberry Crumble
- Bourbon Tiramisu
- Bourbon Maple Cinnamon Rolls
- Bourbon Soufflé
- Bourbon Cheesecake
- Bourbon Strawberry Shortcakes
- Frozen Bourbon Affogato
- Bourbon Caramel Corn with Toasted Pecans

Citrus & Sin (Orange Curd Tart)

Bright, tangy curd in a buttery shell, kissed with bourbon for a tart that's as bold as it is elegant.

Ingredients

(makes one 9-inch tart)

Crust	Filling & Topping
1 ¼ cups (150g) all-purpose flour	½ cup (120ml) fresh orange juice
½ cup (115g) unsalted butter, cold	2 tbsp bourbon
⅓ cup (65g) sugar	3 large eggs
¼ tsp salt	½ cup (100g) sugar
2–3 tbsp ice water	2 tbsp unsalted butter
	Zest of 1 orange

Instructions

1. Make the crust: Cut butter into flour, sugar, and salt until crumbly. Add ice water, form a dough, chill 30 minutes. Roll out and blind bake at 375°F (190°C) for 20 minutes.
2. Whisk orange juice, zest, sugar, eggs, and bourbon in a saucepan over medium heat until thickened. Stir in butter.
3. Pour curd into cooled crust. Chill until set, about 2 hours.

Bourbon Pairings

- *Angel's Envy*: its orange peel notes echo the tart's citrus zing.
- *Woodford Reserve Double Oaked*: creamy vanilla and caramel play well against silky curd.
- *Buffalo Trace*: crisp spice and sweetness make a balanced backdrop.

Cocktail Pairing – Bourbon Sidecar

Shake 2 oz bourbon, 1 oz Cointreau, ¾ oz lemon juice with ice. Strain into a sugar-rimmed coupe.

Who knew sin could taste this bright?

Midnight Barrel (Dark Chocolate Torte)

Dense, fudgy, and unapologetically rich — a chocolate lover's midnight rendezvous with bourbon.

Ingredients

Base	Ganache
8 oz (225g) dark chocolate	4 oz (115g) dark chocolate
½ cup (115g) unsalted butter	½ cup (120ml) heavy cream
¾ cup (150g) sugar	1 tbsp bourbon
¼ tsp salt	
3 large eggs	
1 tsp vanilla	

Instructions

1. Melt chocolate and butter together. Stir in sugar, salt, vanilla, and bourbon.
2. Beat in eggs one at a time. Pour into greased 9-inch pan. Bake 25 minutes at 350°F (175°C). Cool.
3. Heat cream, pour over chocolate, whisk smooth. Spread ganache on cooled cake.

Bourbon Pairings

- *Maker's Mark Cask Strength*: amplifies chocolate with bold caramel.
- *Elijah Craig Small Batch*: oak and cocoa are natural partners.
- *Four Roses Single Barrel*: fruit notes add intrigue to the richness.

Cocktail Pairing – Espresso Bourbon Martini

Shake 2 oz bourbon, 1 oz espresso, ½ oz coffee liqueur, ½ oz simple syrup with ice. Strain into a martini glass.

Midnight snacks, but make it scandalous.

Cotta in the Act (Blood Orange Panna Cotta)

Silky cream set with citrus and bourbon — proof that being caught red-handed can be delicious.

Ingredients

Panna Cotta

2 cups (480ml) heavy cream

½ cup (120ml) whole milk

½ cup (100g) sugar

1 tbsp bourbon

1 packet (7g) gelatin

Zest of 1 blood orange

Sauce

½ cup (120ml) blood orange juice

¼ cup (50g) sugar

1 tbsp bourbon

1 tsp cornstarch

Instructions

1. Sprinkle gelatin over milk; let bloom. Heat cream, sugar, zest, and bourbon until steaming. Stir in gelatin until dissolved. Pour into ramekins; chill until set (4 hrs).
2. Simmer juice, sugar, bourbon, and cornstarch until syrupy. Cool and drizzle over panna cotta.

Bourbon Pairings

- *Knob Creek*: high-proof backbone cuts through cream.
- *Bulleit Bourbon*: citrus-friendly spice mirrors blood orange brightness.
- *Eagle Rare 10 Year*: refined vanilla smooths the finish.

Cocktail Pairing – Boulevardier

Stir 1 oz bourbon, 1 oz Campari, 1 oz sweet vermouth with ice. Strain into a rocks glass over a large cube.

Caught red-handed, but deliciously so.

Raspberry Flame (Baked Alaska)

Layers of cake, ice cream, and flame-kissed meringue — bourbon makes this showstopper burn brighter.

Ingredients

Cake	Meringue & Assembly
½ cup (65g) flour	3 large egg whites
½ tsp baking powder	½ cup (100g) sugar
2 large eggs	1 pint raspberry sorbet
½ cup (100g) sugar	1 pint vanilla ice cream
¼ cup (60ml) milk	2 tbsp bourbon
1 tbsp bourbon	

Instructions

1. Bake sponge cake base at 350°F (175°C) for 15 minutes; cool.
2. Place sorbet and ice cream layers on cake; freeze solid.
3. Whip egg whites and sugar to stiff peaks. Spread meringue around frozen cake.
4. Torch meringue or bake at 500°F (260°C) for 3 minutes. Splash bourbon over and flambé for drama.

Bourbon Pairings

- *Wild Turkey 101*: bold enough to stand against fire and sweetness.
- *Old Forester 1920*: chocolatey depth balances fruit.
- *Blanton's*: smooth elegance complements the finish.

Cocktail Pairing – Raspberry Bourbon Smash

Muddle raspberries, ½ oz lemon juice, and ½ oz simple syrup. Add 2 oz bourbon, shake, strain over crushed ice.

Dessert and pyrotechnics, all in one bite.

The Banana Stand (Banana Upside-Down Cake)

Caramelized bananas, bourbon drizzle, and golden cake flipped into pure comfort.

Ingredients

Caramel Base

½ cup (100g) brown sugar

¼ cup (60g) butter

2 tbsp bourbon

3 bananas, sliced

Cake

1 ½ cups (190g) flour

1 tsp baking powder

½ tsp baking soda

½ tsp salt

½ cup (115g) butter

¾ cup (150g) sugar

2 eggs

½ cup (120ml) sour cream

2 tbsp bourbon

Instructions

1. Melt butter, sugar, and bourbon in skillet; arrange banana slices in caramel.
2. Beat cake ingredients; pour batter over bananas.
3. Bake at 350°F (175°C) for 40–45 minutes. Invert onto plate while warm.

Bourbon Pairings

- *Basil Hayden*: light spice enhances banana's natural sweetness.
- *1792 Small Batch*: caramel-toffee notes play with the upside-down caramel.
- *Jefferson's Reserve*: a smooth, elegant partner for a homestyle classic.

Cocktail Pairing – Banana Bourbon Milkshake

Blend 2 scoops vanilla ice cream, ½ banana, 2 oz bourbon, splash of milk. Garnish with whipped cream.

There's always money in this cake.

Hole Lotta Bourbon (Glazed Donuts)

Caramelized bananas, bourbon drizzle, and golden cake flipped into pure comfort.

Ingredients

(makes 12 donuts)

Donuts

2 ¼ tsp (1 packet) yeast

¾ cup (180ml) warm milk

2 tbsp sugar

3 ½ cups (420g) flour

2 tbsp butter, melted

1 tsp salt

2 eggs

Oil, for frying

Glaze

1 ½ cups (190g) powdered sugar

3–4 tbsp bourbon

1–2 tbsp milk

Instructions

1. Proof yeast in warm milk with sugar. Stir in eggs, butter, salt, and flour; knead until smooth. Let rise 1 hour.
2. Roll dough ½-inch thick, cut rounds, rest 30 minutes.
3. Fry at 350°F (175°C) until golden, 1–2 minutes per side.
4. Whisk glaze ingredients and dip warm donuts.

Bourbon Pairings

- *Maker's Mark*: its sweet wheat base matches the sugar glaze.
- *Wild Turkey 101*: high proof cuts through fried richness.
- *Old Forester*: caramel and vanilla mirror donut vibes.

Cocktail Pairing – Bourbon Cream Coffee

Stir 1 oz bourbon cream liqueur into hot coffee, top with whipped cream.

A hole-in-one way to start the day.

Bourbon Snickerdoodles

Soft, chewy, cinnamon-dusted cookies that trade milk for a dram of bourbon.

Ingredients

(makes 24 cookies)

Dough	Coating
½ cup (115g) butter	2 tbsp sugar
¾ cup (150g) sugar	1 tsp cinnamon
1 egg	
1 tbsp bourbon	
1 tsp vanilla	
1 ½ cups (180g) flour	
½ tsp cream of tartar	
½ tsp baking soda	
¼ tsp salt	

Instructions

1. Cream butter and sugar. Add egg, bourbon, and vanilla.
2. Mix in dry ingredients. Chill 30 minutes (or don't, rebel).
3. Roll into balls, coat in cinnamon sugar. Bake 10 minutes at 350°F (175°C).

Bourbon Pairings

- *Larceny*: wheated softness hugs the cinnamon spice.
- *Bulleit*: a bit of rye spice balances the sugar.
- *Buffalo Trace*: smooth caramel finish for a cozy pairing.

Cocktail Pairing – Bourbon Hot Toddy

Mix 2 oz bourbon, 1 tbsp honey, ½ lemon, and hot water. Stir with a cinnamon stick.

The devil's work never tasted so sweet.

Cast Iron Kiss (Skillet Cookie)

Crisp edges, gooey center, and bourbon baked right into the dough — this cookie is a love letter to comfort.

Ingredients

Cookie Base

1 cup (225g) butter, melted

1 cup (200g) brown sugar

½ cup (100g) sugar

2 eggs

2 tbsp bourbon

2 cups (240g) flour

1 tsp baking soda

½ tsp salt

Mix-Ins (optional)

1 cup (175g) chocolate chips

½ cup (75g) chopped pecans

Instructions

1. Stir butter, sugars, eggs, and bourbon. Add dry ingredients.
2. Fold in chocolate chips and/or pecans.
3. Spread into cast iron skillet. Bake at 350°F (175°C) for 25–30 minutes.

Bourbon Pairings

- *Woodford Reserve*: full-bodied oak and vanilla meet gooey cookie edges.
- *Eagle Rare*: caramel and toffee elevate the sweetness.
- *Elijah Craig*: smoky spice against chocolate richness.

Cocktail Pairing – Bourbon Milk Punch

Shake 2 oz bourbon, 1 oz milk, ½ oz vanilla syrup, ¼ tsp nutmeg with ice. Strain into glass.

Crisp edge, gooey center—cookie therapy in cast iron.

Easy Does It (No-Bake Mousse Cups)

Whipped, rich, and ready in minutes — these mousse cups are the no-fuss, high-reward heroes of dessert.

Ingredients
(makes 6 cups)

Mousse	Topping
1 cup (240ml) heavy cream	Whipped cream
8 oz (225g) dark chocolate	Chocolate shavings
¼ cup (60ml) bourbon	Fresh berries
2 tbsp sugar	
1 tsp vanilla	

Instructions

1. Melt chocolate, stir in bourbon, sugar, and vanilla.
2. Whip cream to soft peaks. Fold into chocolate mixture.
3. Spoon into cups, chill 2 hours. Top with whipped cream and garnish.

Bourbon Pairings

- *Maker's Mark 46*: spice and vanilla elevate mousse depth.
- *Angel's Envy*: its port finish matches berry garnish.
- *Knob Creek*: bold oak cuts through chocolate.

Cocktail Pairing – Bourbon Berry Fizz
Muddle berries with ½ oz simple syrup. Add 2 oz bourbon, top with soda water.

Proof that dessert doesn't always need an oven.

Bourbon-Pecan Shortbread Bars

Buttery shortbread topped with nutty bourbon caramel — pie's casual, easy-going cousin.

Ingredients

Base	Topping
1 cup (225g) butter	1 ½ cups (180g) pecans, chopped
½ cup (100g) sugar	½ cup (100g) brown sugar
2 cups (240g) flour	¼ cup (60ml) bourbon
½ tsp salt	¼ cup (60g) butter
	¼ cup (60ml) cream

Instructions

1. Mix base ingredients, press into 9x13 pan. Bake 15 minutes at 350°F (175°C).
2. Simmer butter, brown sugar, bourbon, and cream. Stir in pecans.
3. Pour topping over base, bake 15 more minutes. Cool before cutting.

Bourbon Pairings

- *Wild Turkey Rare Breed*: spicy and bold, stands against sweet nut topping.
- *Russell's Reserve 10*: nutty oak mirrors pecans.
- *Basil Hayden*: delicate spice, easy-drinking balance.

Cocktail Pairing – Pecan Old Fashioned

Muddle 1 sugar cube with 2 dashes bitters and a splash of pecan syrup. Add 2 oz bourbon, stir with ice, garnish with orange peel.

Like pecan pie, but portable (and bourboned).

Whiskey Brownies

Dark, fudgy brownies with a bourbon glaze — chocolate with a dangerous streak.

Ingredients

Brownies

1 cup (225g) butter

8 oz (225g) dark chocolate

1 ½ cups (300g) sugar

4 eggs

1 tsp vanilla

¾ cup (90g) flour

½ cup (50g) cocoa powder

½ tsp salt

Bourbon Glaze

1 cup (120g) powdered sugar

3 tbsp bourbon

1–2 tbsp milk

Instructions

1. Melt butter and chocolate, whisk in sugar.
2. Add eggs and vanilla, then dry ingredients. Pour into greased 9x13 pan.
3. Bake at 350°F (175°C) for 25–30 minutes.
4. Whisk glaze ingredients and drizzle over cooled brownies.

Bourbon Pairings

- *Four Roses Single Barrel*: fruity notes pop against rich cocoa.
- *Old Forester 1920*: high proof stands up to dense chocolate.
- *Heaven Hill 7 Year*: caramelized depth mirrors fudgy bite.

Cocktail Pairing – Bourbon Espresso Martini

Shake 2 oz bourbon, 1 oz coffee liqueur, 1 oz espresso, ½ oz simple syrup with ice. Strain into martini glass.

Brownies are good. Brownies with bourbon? Dangerous.

Bourbon Bread Pudding

Custard-soaked bread baked golden, finished with bourbon sauce — a boozy second life for stale loaves.

Ingredients

Pudding	Bourbon Sauce
6 cups cubed day-old bread	½ cup (100g) sugar
2 cups (480ml) milk	½ cup (115g) butter
1 cup (240ml) cream	½ cup (120ml) bourbon
4 eggs	1 tsp vanilla
1 cup (200g) sugar	
1 tsp cinnamon	
1 tsp vanilla	

Instructions

1. Whisk milk, cream, eggs, sugar, cinnamon, vanilla. Pour over bread cubes. Let soak 30 minutes.
2. Bake at 350°F (175°C) for 40–45 minutes.
3. Simmer sauce ingredients until slightly thickened. Drizzle over warm pudding.

Bourbon Pairings

- *Eagle Rare*: smooth caramel notes match bread custard.
- *Knob Creek*: bold spice complements sweet sauce.
- *Maker's Mark*: mellow wheat character keeps things cozy.

Cocktail Pairing – Bourbon Cream Eggnog (any season)

Shake 2 oz bourbon cream, 1 oz bourbon, 1 egg yolk, ½ oz sugar, and nutmeg. Serve chilled with a dusting of spice.

Proof that stale bread deserves a second life—preferably soused.

Pumpkin Crème Brûlée

Silky pumpkin custard with a caramelized sugar crackle — autumn dressed in bourbon.

Ingredients

(makes 6 ramekins)

Custard	Topping
1 cup (240ml) cream	½ cup (100g) sugar
1 cup (240ml) milk	¼ cup (50g) brown sugar
5 egg yolks	
½ cup (120g) pumpkin purée	
¼ cup (60ml) bourbon	
½ tsp cinnamon	
¼ tsp nutmeg	

Instructions

1. Heat cream, milk, and pumpkin with spices.
2. Whisk yolks and sugar, temper with hot cream mix. Stir in bourbon.
3. Pour into ramekins, bake in water bath at 325°F (160°C) for 35–40 minutes. Chill.
4. Sprinkle sugar on top, torch to crackly perfection.

Bourbon Pairings

- *Buffalo Trace*: pumpkin pie spice meets smooth caramel.
- *Elijah Craig*: oak warmth enhances nutmeg and cinnamon.
- *Angel's Envy*: port finish pairs like Thanksgiving dessert wine.

Cocktail Pairing – Pumpkin Bourbon Sour

Shake 2 oz bourbon, 1 oz lemon juice, 1 oz pumpkin syrup, dash of bitters. Serve over ice with cinnamon stick.

Jack-o'-lanterns wish they ended this sweetly.

Peach Raspberry Crumble

Juicy fruit baked under a crisp, buttery topping — bourbon makes the summer sweetness sing.

Ingredients

Fruit Filling	Crumble Topping
4 peaches, sliced	1 cup (120g) flour
1 cup (125g) raspberries	½ cup (100g) sugar
¼ cup (50g) sugar	½ cup (115g) butter, cubed
2 tbsp bourbon	½ tsp cinnamon

Instructions

1. Toss fruit with sugar and bourbon. Place in baking dish.
2. Mix topping until crumbly. Sprinkle over fruit.
3. Bake at 350°F (175°C) for 35–40 minutes until golden.

Bourbon Pairings

- *Basil Hayden*: delicate spice lifts berry brightness.
- *Woodford Reserve*: stone fruit notes mirror peaches.
- *Wild Turkey 101*: bold enough to play against tart raspberries.

Cocktail Pairing – Bourbon Peach Smash

Muddle peach slices with ½ oz simple syrup. Add 2 oz bourbon, shake with ice, top with soda.

A summer fling between bourbon and fruit.

Bourbon Tiramisu

Coffee, cocoa, mascarpone, and bourbon-soaked ladyfingers — an Italian classic with a Kentucky twist.

Ingredients

Layers	Cream Filling
1 pack ladyfingers	8 oz (225g) mascarpone
1 ½ cups (360ml) coffee, cooled	1 cup (240ml) cream
½ cup (120ml) bourbon	¼ cup (50g) sugar
Cocoa powder	1 tsp vanilla

Instructions

1. Whisk mascarpone, cream, sugar, vanilla until fluffy.
2. Mix coffee with bourbon. Dip ladyfingers quickly, layer in dish.
3. Spread mascarpone mixture over. Repeat layers.
4. Chill 4+ hours. Dust with cocoa before serving.

Bourbon Pairings

- *Jefferson's Ocean*: hints of salinity balance coffee's bitterness.
- *E.H. Taylor Small Batch*: caramel and vanilla smooth out cocoa.
- *Elijah Craig Barrel Proof*: rich punch keeps up with bold coffee.

Cocktail Pairing – Bourbon Affogato (Nightcap Edition)

Pour a shot of espresso over vanilla ice cream, float 1 oz bourbon.

The Italian classic—gone rogue with Kentucky swagger.

Bourbon Maple Cinnamon Rolls

Soft spirals of cinnamon-sugar, glazed with maple-bourbon bliss — breakfast just became dessert.

Ingredients

Dough	Filling	Glaze
4 cups (480g) flour	1 cup (200g) brown sugar	1 cup (120g) powdered sugar
1 cup (240ml) warm milk	2 tbsp cinnamon	2 tbsp maple syrup
2 ¼ tsp yeast	½ cup (115g) butter, softened	2 tbsp bourbon
½ cup (100g) sugar		1–2 tbsp milk
½ cup (115g) butter		
2 eggs		

Instructions

1. Activate yeast in warm milk with sugar. Add butter, eggs, flour. Knead until smooth. Let rise 1 hr.
2. Roll dough into rectangle, spread with butter, brown sugar, cinnamon. Roll up, slice.
3. Place in pan, rise 30 mins. Bake 350°F (175°C) 25–30 mins.
4. Whisk glaze ingredients, drizzle while warm.

Bourbon Pairings

- *Woodford Reserve Double Oaked*: maple richness meets toasted vanilla.
- *Maker's 46*: French oak spice mirrors cinnamon warmth.
- *Old Forester 1910*: dessert-level caramel depth.

Cocktail Pairing – Bourbon Chai Latte

Steep strong chai, stir in 2 oz bourbon, top with steamed milk and honey.

Breakfast is just dessert we don't apologize for.

Bourbon Soufflé

Airy, delicate, and laced with bourbon — a dessert that rises to any occasion.

Ingredients

Base	Meringue
3 tbsp butter	4 egg whites
3 tbsp flour	¼ cup (50g) sugar
1 cup (240ml) milk	
4 egg yolks	
¼ cup (50g) sugar	
2 tbsp bourbon	

Instructions

1. Make roux with butter, flour, milk. Stir in yolks, sugar, bourbon. Cool slightly.
2. Beat whites with sugar to stiff peaks. Fold into base.
3. Pour into buttered ramekins, bake at 375°F (190°C) 15–18 mins. Serve immediately.

Bourbon Pairings

- *Blanton's*: elegance meets airy lift.
- *Angel's Envy*: port finish elevates delicacy.
- *Elmer T. Lee*: refined balance, just like the soufflé.

Cocktail Pairing – Bourbon French 75

Shake 1 oz bourbon, ½ oz lemon, ½ oz simple syrup. Top with Champagne.

Impress your in-laws—or just yourself.

Bourbon Cheesecake

Creamy, decadent, and spiked with bourbon — the cheesecake that doesn't need toppings to impress.

Ingredients

(9-inch springform)

Crust	Filling
1 ½ cups (150g) graham crumbs	24 oz (675g) cream cheese
¼ cup (50g) sugar	1 cup (200g) sugar
6 tbsp butter, melted	3 eggs
	1 cup (240ml) sour cream
	¼ cup (60ml) bourbon
	1 tsp vanilla

Instructions

1. Mix crust, press into pan, bake 10 mins at 325°F (160°C).
2. Beat filling ingredients until smooth. Pour over crust.
3. Bake in water bath 50–55 mins. Chill 4 hrs+.

Bourbon Pairings

- *Eagle Rare*: creamy vanilla heaven.
- *Russell's Reserve 10*: spice kick keeps it lively.
- *Heaven Hill 7*: bourbon-y cheesecake soulmate.

Cocktail Pairing – Bourbon Blackberry Smash

Muddle blackberries + mint, add 2 oz bourbon, ½ oz lemon juice, ½ oz simple. Shake, strain over ice.

This cake doesn't crack—unless you share it too early.

Strawberry Shortcakes with Bourbon Cream

Flaky biscuits stacked with boozy berries and whipped cream — Southern charm in three layers.

Ingredients

Shortcakes	Filling
2 cups (240g) flour	2 cups strawberries, sliced
¼ cup (50g) sugar	2 tbsp sugar
1 tbsp baking powder	2 tbsp bourbon
½ tsp salt	1 cup cream, whipped with 2 tbsp sugar + 1 tbsp bourbon
½ cup (115g) butter	
⅔ cup (160ml) milk	

Instructions

1. Mix dry, cut in butter. Stir in milk. Pat, cut biscuits. Bake 425°F (220°C) 12–15 mins.
2. Toss berries with sugar + bourbon.
3. Split biscuits, fill with berries and bourbon cream.

Bourbon Pairings

- *Bulleit Bourbon*: spicy kick against fresh berries.
- *1792 Small Batch*: fruit-forward bourbon = fruit-forward dessert.
- *Wild Turkey Rare Breed*: bold, yet sweet with cream.

Cocktail Pairing – Strawberry Bourbon Lemonade

Shake 2 oz bourbon, 1 oz lemon, 1 oz strawberry syrup. Top with soda.

Southern charm in three layers—berry, cream, bourbon.

Frozen Bourbon Affogato

Vanilla ice cream drowned in espresso and bourbon — proof that multitasking can be delicious.

Ingredients

Base	Topping
4 scoops vanilla gelato (or ice cream)	4 oz hot espresso
2 oz bourbon	Shaved chocolate or cocoa powder
1 tbsp brown sugar (optional)	Whipped cream (optional)

Instructions

1. Place one scoop gelato into each chilled glass.
2. Stir bourbon and espresso together (add sugar if you like it sweeter).
3. Pour hot mix over the gelato.
4. Sprinkle with chocolate or top with whipped cream. Serve immediately.

Bourbon Pairings

- *Buffalo Trace*: smooth caramel notes match espresso's bitter edge.
- *Four Roses Single Barrel*: floral spice adds complexity to a simple dessert.
- *Jim Beam Black*: affordable, approachable, and coffee's best buddy.

Cocktail Pairing – Espresso Old Fashioned

Stir 2 oz bourbon, ½ oz espresso, ¼ oz simple syrup, 2 dashes bitters over ice. Garnish with orange twist.

Coffee, ice cream, bourbon — this is multitasking at its best.

Bourbon Caramel Corn with Toasted Pecans

Crunchy, sticky, and spiked with bourbon — snack food turned dangerously addictive.

Ingredients

(makes about 10 cups)

Popcorn Base

10 cups popped popcorn

1 cup (100g) toasted pecans

Caramel Sauce

1 cup (200g) brown sugar

½ cup (115g) butter

¼ cup (60ml) corn syrup
2 tbsp bourbon
½ tsp baking soda
1 tsp vanilla

Instructions

1. Preheat oven to 250°F (120°C). Line baking sheet with parchment.
2. Place popcorn + pecans in large bowl.
3. In saucepan, melt butter, sugar, corn syrup. Simmer 5 mins. Stir in bourbon, soda, vanilla.
4. Pour over popcorn, toss well. Spread on sheet.
5. Bake 45 mins, stirring every 15. Cool, break apart.

Bourbon Pairings

- *Wild Turkey 101*: bold enough to hold its own against sticky sweetness.
- *Evan Williams Bottled-in-Bond*: budget-friendly caramel-on-caramel action.
- *Knob Creek 9*: smoky char contrasts the buttery crunch.

Cocktail Pairing – Bourbon Mule

Shake 2 oz bourbon, ½ oz lime, ½ oz simple syrup. Pour over ice, top with ginger beer.

Sweet, salty, boozy crunch — good luck stopping at one handful.

A Collector's Pour

A Spirited Side Note

Welcome to the part of the book where I show you what happens when a hobby spirals into a lifestyle.

You've tasted the recipes. You've read the bourbon notes. But here's a peek behind the curtain—or more accurately, behind the cabinet doors. What started as a casual love of whiskey turned into full-blown bourbon hunting. A bottle here, a bottle there, and suddenly I had a "collection" (which is what I started calling it when my mom asked questions). And because I believe in full transparency—and because my shelves are out of room anyway—I figured it was time to show you the heart of the home: the bourbon wall.

My collection includes the bold, the smooth, the small batch, the limited release, the oddly shaped, and yes—the ones I bought just for the label. There are bottles I cook with, bottles I save for guests, and bottles that are strictly "emotional support bourbon." I've got more Elijah Craig than I'm willing to admit on paper, and if you spot duplicates, no you didn't.

Let the record show: the rum shelf? That one's my husband's. I may have started it so I'd feel less guilty buying bourbon, and I occasionally toss him a collector bottle to keep the peace. The H. Deringer bottles, the Doc Holliday pour, and the very dramatic Bourbon Pistol Set? His. He loves guns, the Tombstone movie, and anything that comes in a case with hinges. Our son even bought him a glass that says, "I'll be your huckleberry."

My mom still asks if I'm drinking all of this (I'm not), and no one's allowed to ask my husband what any of it is worth (he doesn't know, and let's keep it that way). But every bottle here means something—even if that something is, "I found this on sale and screamed."

So here it is: the lineup, the legacy, the proof (literally). Whether it's a dusty bottle I hunted for months or one I cracked open on a Tuesday just because it felt right, this collection isn't just for looking at. It's for living with, cooking with, and sharing with the people I love.

And if you're a distillery reading this: I am very available for sponsorships. Call me.

A Note from the Author

If you've made it this far, first of all — thank you. Truly. Thank you for indulging me in what has become a wildly indulgent hobby: collecting bourbon, cooking with bourbon, writing about bourbon, and convincing people that yes, it really does belong in everything from mashed potatoes to dessert sauce. You didn't have to come along for the ride, but I'm so glad you did.

This book started as a simple idea: what if I took two of my great loves — bourbon and cooking — and let them meet in the middle? Turns out, that "middle" is a crowded kitchen with a cabinet full of whiskey, a counter covered in flour, a dog sniffing suspiciously at the oven, and me whispering "just one more splash" while my mother texts me again asking if I've joined a tasting club or a support group. (The answer is still: neither. But if there's a third option where we eat bourbon-glazed short ribs and call it therapy, sign me up.)

Food has always been my love language. It's how I celebrate, how I cope, how I connect. I'm the type who shows up with a pan of something warm when you're hurting, or drops off cookies "just because." So when I say I wrote this book to share something I love — I mean it in the most literal way. These recipes aren't just meals. They're moments. They're cozy nights, clinking glasses, sticky fingers, and laughter echoing down the hallway. They're second helpings and no regrets.

And yes — most of them include bourbon. Because to me, bourbon adds more than flavor. It adds depth. It adds to the story. It adds that slow, smoky hush that reminds you to pause between bites and enjoy the experience. And let's be honest — it also adds a little swagger to the stovetop, which never hurts.

So whether you're a whiskey collector, a curious cook, or someone who just likes a good sauce and a reason to pour a drink — this book is for you.

Thanks for pulling up a chair at The Bourbon Table. Now take a bottle from the shelf, call your mama, and go make something worth remembering.

Cheers,

Jocelyn

www.ingramcontent.com/pod-product-compliance
Lightning Source LLC
Chambersburg PA
CBHW041145120626
46547CB00020B/3117